50 Leveled Math Problems

150 Problems Total

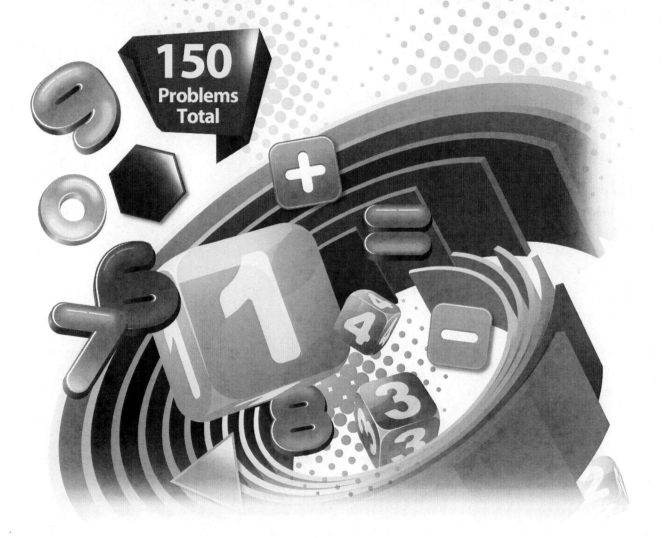

Author

Linda Dacey, Ed.D.

LESLEY
UNIVERSITY

SHELL EDUCATION

Contributing Author and Consultant

Anne M. Collins, Ph.D.
Director of Mathematics Programs
Director of Achievement Center
  for Mathematics
Lesley University

Consultants

Jayne Bamford Lynch, M.Ed.
National Faculty
Lesley University

Fredi Hurwitz, M.Ed.
Grade 1 Teacher
Cambridge Public Schools

Amy Molyan, M.Ed.
Grade 1 Teacher
Cambridge Public Schools

Publishing Credits

Dona Herweck Rice, *Editor-in-Chief*; Robin Erickson, *Production Director*;
Lee Aucoin, *Creative Director*; Timothy J. Bradley, *Illustration Manager*;
Sara Johnson, M.S.Ed., *Senior Editor*; Aubrie Nielsen, M.S.Ed., *Associate Education Editor*;
Leah Quillian, *Assistant Editor*; Grace Alba, *Interior Layout Designer*; Agi Palinay, *Illustrator*;
Corinne Burton, M.A.Ed., *Publisher*

Standards
© 2003 National Council of Teachers of Mathematics (NCTM)
© 2004 Mid-continent Research for Education and Learning (McREL)
© 2007 Teachers of English to Speakers of Other Languages, Inc. (TESOL)
© 2010 National Governors Association Center for Best Practices and Council of Chief State School Officers (CCSS)

Shell Education

5301 Oceanus Drive
Huntington Beach, CA 92649-1030
http://www.shelleducation.com
ISBN 978-1-4258-0773-3
© 2012 Shell Educational Publishing, Inc.

Reprinted 2013

Table of Contents

Introduction

Leveled Problem-Solving Lessons

Operations and Algebraic Thinking

Number and Operations in Base Ten

Table of Contents (cont.)

Problem Solving in Mathematics Instruction

If you were a student in elementary school before the early 1980s, your education most likely paid little or no attention to mathematical problem solving. In fact, your exposure may have been limited to solving word problems at the end of a chapter that focused on one of the four operations. After a chapter on addition, for example, you solved problems that required you to add two numbers to find the answer. You knew this was the case, so you just picked out the two numbers from the problem and added them. Sometimes, but rarely, you were assigned problems that required you to choose whether to add, subtract, multiply, or divide. Many of your teachers dreaded lessons that contained such problems as they did not know how to help the many students who struggled.

If you went to elementary school in the later 1980s or in the 1990s, it may have been different. You may have learned about a four-step model of problem solving and perhaps you were introduced to different strategies for finding solutions. There may have been a separate chapter in your textbook that focused on problem solving and two-page lessons that focused on particular problem-solving strategies, such as guess and check. Attention was given to problems that required more than one computational step for their solution, and all the information necessary to solve the problems was not necessarily contained in the problem statements.

One would think that the ability of students to solve problems would improve greatly with these changes, but that has not been the case. Research provides little evidence that teaching problem solving in this isolated manner leads to success (Cai 2010). In fact, some would argue that valuable instructional time was lost exploring problems that did not match the mathematical goals of the curriculum. An example would be learning how to use logic tables to solve a problem that involved finding out who drank which drink and wore which color shirt. Being able to use a diagram to organize information, to reason deductively, and to eliminate possibilities are all important problem-solving skills, but they should be applied to problems that are mathematically significant and interesting to students.

Today, leaders in mathematics education recommend teaching mathematics in a manner that integrates attention to concepts, skills, and mathematical reasoning. Referred to as *teaching through problem solving,* this approach suggests that problematic tasks serve as vehicles through which students acquire new mathematical concepts and skills (D'Ambrosio 2003). Students apply previous learning and gain new insights into mathematics as they wrestle with challenging tasks. This approach is quite different from introducing problems only after content has been learned.

Most recently, the *Common Core State Standards* listed the need to persevere in problem solving as the first of its Standards for Mathematical Practice (National Governors Association Center for Best Practices and Council of Chief State School Officers 2010):

> **Make sense of problems and persevere in solving them.**
> *Mathematically proficient students start by explaining to themselves the meaning of a problem and looking for entry points to its solution. They analyze givens, constraints, relationships, and goals. They make conjectures about the form and meaning of the solution and plan a solution pathway rather than simply jumping into a solution attempt. They consider analogous problems, and try special cases and simpler forms of the original problem in order to gain*

Problem Solving in Mathematics Instruction *(cont.)*

insight into its solution. They monitor and evaluate their progress and change course if necessary. Older students might, depending on the context of the problem, transform algebraic expressions or change the viewing window on their graphing calculator to get the information they need. Mathematically proficient students can explain correspondences between equations, verbal descriptions, tables, and graphs or draw diagrams of important features and relationships, graph data, and search for regularity or trends. Younger students might rely on using concrete objects or pictures to help conceptualize and solve a problem. Mathematically proficient students check their answers to problems using a different method, and they continually ask themselves, "Does this make sense?" They can understand the approaches of others to solving complex problems and identify correspondences between different approaches.

This sustained commitment to problem solving makes sense; it is the application of mathematical skills to real-life problems that makes learning mathematics so important. Unfortunately, we have not yet mastered the art of developing successful problem solvers. Students' performance in the United States on the 2009 Program for International Student Assessment (PISA), a test that evaluates 15-year-old students' mathematical literacy and ability to apply mathematics to real-life situations, suggests that we need to continue to improve our teaching of mathematical problem solving. According to data released late in 2010, students in the U.S. are below average (National Center for Educational Statistics 2010). Clearly we need to address this lack of success.

Students do not have enough opportunities to solve challenging problems. Further, problems available to teachers are not designed to meet the individual needs of students. Additionally, teachers have few opportunities to learn how best to create, identify, and orchestrate problem-solving tasks. *50 Leveled Math Problems* is a unique series that is designed to address these concerns.

Understanding the Problem-Solving Process

George Polya is known as the father of problem solving. In his book *How to Solve It: A New Aspect of Mathematical Method* (1945), Polya provides a four-step model of problem solving that has been adopted in many classrooms: understanding the problem, making a plan, carrying out the plan, and looking back. In some elementary classrooms this model has been shortened to: understand, plan, do, check. Unfortunately, this over-simplification ignores much of the richness of Polya's thinking.

Polya's conceptual model of the problem-solving process has been adapted for use at this level. Teachers are encouraged to view the four steps as interrelated, rather than only sequential, and to recognize that problem-solving strategies are useful at each stage of the problem-solving process. The model presented here gives greater emphasis to the importance of communicating and justifying one's thinking as well as to posing problems. Ways in which understanding is deepened throughout the problem-solving process is considered in each of the following steps.

Step 1: Understand the Problem

Students engage in the problem-solving process when they attempt to *understand the problem*, but the understanding is not something that just happens in the beginning. At grade 1, the teacher may read the problem aloud several times to support emerging readers. Students may be asked to restate the problem in their own words and then turn to a neighbor to summarize what they know and what they need to find out. At this grade level, it is important for students to be able to visualize or model the problem.

What is most important is that teachers do not teach students to rely on key words or show students "tricks" or "short-cuts" that are not built on conceptual understanding. Interpreting the language of mathematics is complex, and terms that are used in mathematics often have different everyday meanings. Note how a reliance on key words would lead to failure when solving the following problem. A student taught that *left* means *subtract* may decide that 10 – 6, or 4 steps, is the correct answer.

> *Melissa walked 10 steps.*
> *Then she turned to the left and walked 6 more steps.*
> *How many steps did Melissa walk?*

Ways in which understanding is deepened throughout the problem-solving process is considered in each of the following steps.

Understanding the Problem-Solving Process *(cont.)*

Step 2: Apply Strategies

Once students have a sense of the problem they can begin to actively explore it. They may do so by applying one or more of the strategies below. Note that related actions are combined within some of the strategies.

- Act it out or use manipulatives.
- Count, compute, or write an equation.
- Find information in a picture, list, table, graph, or diagram.
- Generalize a pattern.
- Guess and check or make an estimate.

- Organize information in a picture, list, table, graph, or diagram.
- Simplify the problem.
- Use logical reasoning.
- Work backward.

As students apply these strategies, they also deepen their understanding of the *mathematics* of the problem. As such, understanding develops throughout the problem-solving phases. Consider the following problem requiring students to write the numbers in the blanks so that the story makes sense.

Use each number in the box once to fill in the blanks.

6	2	8	3

All About Jed
Jed has _____ brothers.
Jed has _____ sisters.
Jed has more brothers than sisters.
There are _____ children in Jed's family.
There are _____ people in Jed's family.

Chloé and Rake are working together. They have read the problem and understand that they are to write the numbers so that the story makes sense. When Rake says, "The numbers could go anywhere," Chloé responds, "Okay, let's do it." They try two brothers and three sisters. Then they reread the third line of the problem and Rake says, "Wait, the number of brothers has to be more." By making a guess and checking it, Chloé and Rake came to *understand* the necessary relationship among the numbers they chose and the related information in the text.

It is important that we offer students problems that can be solved in more than one way. If one strategy does not lead to success, students can try a different one. This option gives students the opportunity to learn that getting "stuck" might just mean that a new approach should be considered. When students get themselves "unstuck" they are more likely to view themselves as successful problem solvers. Such problems also lead to richer mathematical conversations as there are different ideas and perspectives to discuss.

Understanding the Problem-Solving Process *(cont.)*

Step 2: Apply Strategies *(cont.)*

Consider the following problem:

> *Jillian buys 13 candles.*
> *Some of the candles are red.*
> *The other 6 candles are blue.*
> *How many candles are red?*
> _____ *candles*
> *Write an equation for this problem.*

Consider the student response shown below in Student Sample 1. The student began by drawing an estimated number of candles. If you look closely you can see the extra candles he erased after he counted to check that he drew 13. Using the information given in the problem, he recorded a *b* in the first six candles. He then counted the remaining candles and recorded an *r* in each of them. He recorded an equation to represent the situation. He also provided a written explanation of his thinking. His strategy, equation, and written explanation all suggest the same way of thinking about this problem.

Student Sample 1

As appropriate to the problem's context, his work does not suggest either a joining or a separation of objects; there are merely two parts of the group of candles.

Understanding the Problem-Solving Process *(cont.)*

Step 2: Apply Strategies *(cont.)*

As you can see in Student Sample 2, some students will think in terms of addition to find the number of red candles. This student also does not rely on a drawing. As she indicates, she uses a mental model of the six and then counts up to thirteen, using her fingers to keep track of how many she counts. She then represents this process with an equation.

Student Sample 2

Step 3: Communicate and Justify Your Thinking

It is essential that teachers ask students to communicate and justify their thinking. It is also important that students make records as they work so that they can recall their thinking. When teachers make it clear that they expect such behavior from students, they are establishing an important habit of mind (Goldenberg, Shteingold, and Feurzeig 2003) and developing their understanding of the nature of mathematics. When students explain their thinking orally while investigating a problem with a partner or small group, they may deepen their understanding of the problem or recognize an error and fix it. When students debrief after finding solutions, they learn to communicate their thinking clearly and in ways that give others access to new mathematical ideas. In one class a second-grader listens to a peer's explanation and proclaims, "So you made a number line to figure it out. I'm going to try that." Such discourse is essential to the mathematical practice suggested in the *Common Core State Standards* that students, "construct viable justifications and critique the reasoning of others (National Governors Association Center for Best Practices and Council of Chief State School Officers 2010).

Our task is to foster learning environments where students engage in this kind of *accountable talk*. Michaels, O'Connor, and Resnick (2008) identify three aspects of this type of dialogue. The first is that students are accountable to their learning communities; they listen to each other carefully and build on the ideas of others. Second, accountable talk is based on logical thinking and leads to logical

Understanding the Problem-Solving Process *(cont.)*

Step 3: Communicate and Justify Your Thinking *(cont.)*

conclusions. Finally, these types of discussions are based on facts or other information that is available to everyone.

When we emphasize the importance of discussions and explanations, we are teaching our students that it is the soundness of their mathematical reasoning that determines what is correct, not merely an answer key or a teacher's approval. Students learn, therefore, that mathematics makes sense and that they are mathematical sense-makers.

Step 4: Take It Further

Debrief

It is this final step in the problem-solving process to which teachers and students are most likely to give the least attention. When time is given to this step, it is often limited to "check your work." In contrast, this step offers rich opportunities for further learning. Students might be asked to solve the problem using a different strategy, or to find additional solutions. They might be asked to make a mathematical generalization based on their investigation. Students might connect this problem to another problem they have solved already, or they now may be able to solve a new, higher-level problem.

Posing Problems

Students can also take problem solving further by posing problems. In fact, problem posing is intricately linked with problem solving (Brown and Walter 2005). When posing their own problems, students can view a problem as something they can create, rather than as a task that is given to them. This book supports problem posing through a variety of formats. For example, students may be asked to supply missing data in a problem so that it makes sense. They may be given a problem with the solution omitted and asked to compose one. Or, they may be given both problem data and the answer and asked to identify the missing question. Teachers may also choose to ask students to create their own problems that are similar to those they have previously solved. Emphasis on problem posing can transform the teaching of problem solving and build lifelong curiosity in students. Consider the following reflections of Amy Molyan, a first grade teacher, after she explored *Ask a Question* (page 60) with her students.

> *In the past, as a way of extending a lesson, I have asked my first graders to write their own word problems. Typically, they are very excited to do this. They think of a context easily and enjoy playing around with using really large numbers. They often share that using large numbers will make the problem really hard. So hard, in fact, that they struggle to solve the problems themselves! I have also noticed that most first graders write a story problem but do not actually include a problem to solve; that is, there is no question at the end.*
> *I was intrigued to try the problem-solving lesson Ask a Question. I was wondering if the first graders would find this enjoyable and challenging. I saw it as an opportunity to differentiate since there were many access points to the*

Understanding the Problem-Solving Process (cont.)

Step 4: Take It Further (cont.)

Posing Problems (cont.)

problems. I introduced the problems to the whole group and then reinforced the vocabulary and problems to small groups of children, matching the math level of the child to the appropriate problem. This was a very different way of thinking for most of my students and they called it "the backward way." Thinking of a question that would finish the problem felt backward to them since the question was not there for them to answer.

As I reflect back to my earlier attempts to differentiate by asking first graders to write story problems, I realize that something was missing. Having used this problem-solving lesson, I now can think of places within my own curriculum where I can leave the question off of problems. I never really thought about this before. It opens up many more avenues.

Problem-Solving Strategies

Think of someone doing repair jobs around the house. Often that person carries a toolbox or wears a tool belt from task to task. Common tools such as hammers, screwdrivers, and wrenches are then readily available. The repair person chooses tools (usually more than one) appropriate for a particular task. Problem-solving strategies are the tools used to solve problems. Labeling the strategies allows students to refer to them in discussions and helps students recognize the wide variety of tools available for the solution of problems. The problems in this book provide opportunities for students to apply one or more of the following strategies:

Act It Out or Use Manipulatives

Students' understanding of a problem is greatly enhanced when they act it out. Students may choose to dramatize a situation themselves or use manipulatives to show the actions or changes that take place. If students suggest they do not understand a problem say something such as *Imagine this is a play. Show me what the actors are doing.*

Count, Compute, or Write an Equation

When students count, compute, or write an equation to solve a problem they are making a match between a context and a mathematical skill. Once the connection is made, students need only to carry out the procedure accurately. Sometimes writing an equation is a final step in the solution process. For example, students might work with manipulatives or draw pictures and then summarize their thinking by recording an equation.

Find Information in a Picture, List, Table, Graph, or Diagram

Too often problems contain all of the necessary information in the problem statement. Such information is never so readily available in real-world situations. It is important that students develop the ability to interpret a picture, list, table, graph, or diagram and identify the information relevant to the problem.

Generalize a Pattern

Some people consider mathematics the study of patterns, so it makes sense that the ability to identify, continue, and generalize patterns is an important problem-solving strategy. The ability to generalize a pattern requires students to recognize and express relationships. Once generalized, the student can use the pattern to predict other outcomes.

Guess and Check or Make an Estimate

Guessing and checking or making an estimate provide students with insights into problems. Making a guess can help students to better understand conditions of the problem; it can be a way to try something when a student is stuck. Some students may make random guesses, but over time, students learn to make more informed guesses. For example, if a guess leads to an answer that is too large, a student might next try a number that is less than the previous guess. Estimation can help students narrow their range of guesses or be used to check a guess.

Problem-Solving Strategies *(cont.)*

Organize Information in a Picture, List, Table, Graph, or Diagram

Organizing information can help students both understand and solve problems. For example, students might draw a number line or a map to note information given in the problem statement. When students organize data in a table or graph they might recognize relationships among the data. Students might also make an organized list to keep track of guesses they have made or to identify patterns. It is important that students gather data from a problem and organize it in a way that makes the most sense to them.

Simplify the Problem

Another way for students to better understand a problem, or perhaps get "unstuck," is to simplify it. Often the easiest way for students to do this is to make the numbers easier. For example, a student might replace four-digit numbers with single-digit numbers or replace fractions with whole numbers. With simpler numbers students often gain insights or recognize relationships that were not previously apparent, but that can now be applied to the original problem. Students might also work with 10 numbers, rather than 100, to identify patterns.

Use Logical Reasoning

Logical thinking and sense-making pervade mathematical problem solving. To solve problems students need to deduce relationships, draw conclusions, make inferences, and eliminate possibilities. Logical reasoning is also a component of many other strategies. For example, students use logical reasoning to revise initial guesses or to interpret diagrams. Asking questions such as *What else does this sentence tell you?* helps students to more closely analyze given data.

Work Backward

When the outcome of a situation is known, we often work backward to determine how to arrive at that goal. We might use this strategy to figure out what time to leave for the airport when we know the time our flight is scheduled to depart. A student might work backward to answer the question *What did Joey add to 79 to get a sum of 146?* or *If it took 2 hours and 23 minutes to drive a given route and the driver arrived at 10:17, at what time did the driver leave home?* Understanding relationships among the operations is critical to the successful use of this strategy.

Ask, Don't Tell

All teachers want their students to succeed, and it can be difficult to watch them struggle. Often when students struggle with a problem, a first instinct may be to step in and show them how to solve it. That intervention might feel good, but it is not helpful to the student. Students need to learn how to struggle through the problem-solving process if they are to enhance their understanding and reasoning skills. Perseverance in solving problems is listed under the mathematical practices in the *Common Core State Standards* and research indicates that students who struggle and persevere in solving problems are more likely to internalize the problem-solving process and build upon their successes. It is also important to recognize the fact that people think differently about how to approach and solve problems.

An effective substitution for telling or showing students how to solve problems is to offer support through questioning. George Bright and Jeane Joyner (2005) identify three different types of questions to ask, depending on where students are in the problem-solving process: (1) engaging questions, (2) refocusing questions, and (3) clarifying questions.

Engaging Questions

Engaging questions are designed to pique student interest in a problem. Students are more likely to want to solve problems that are interesting and relevant. One way to immediately grab a student's attention is by using his or her name in the problem. Once a personal connection is made, a student is more apt to persevere in solving the problem. Posing an engaging question is also a great way to redirect a student who is not involved in a group discussion. Suppose students are provided the missing numbers in a problem and one of the sentences reads *Janel is about _____ centimeters tall and rides her bicycle to school.* Engaging questions might include *What do you know about 100 centimeters? Are you taller or shorter than 100 centimeters?* The responses will provide further insight into how the student is thinking.

Refocusing Questions

Refocusing questions are asked to redirect students away from a nonproductive line of thinking and back to a more appropriate track. These questions often begin with the phrase *What can you tell me about…?* or *What does this number…?* Refocusing questions are also appropriate if you suspect students have misread or misunderstood the problem. Asking them to explain in their own words what the problem is stating and what question they are trying to answer is often helpful.

Clarifying Questions

Clarifying questions are posed when it is unclear why students have used a certain strategy, picture, table, graph, or computation. They are designed to help demonstrate what students are thinking, but can also be used to clear up misconceptions students might have. The teacher might say *I am not sure why you started with the number 10. Can you explain that to me?*

As teachers transform instruction from "teaching as telling" to "teaching as facilitating," students may require an adjustment period to become accustomed to the change in expectations. Over time, students will learn to take more responsibility and to expect the teacher to probe their thinking, rather than supply them with answers. After making this transition in her own teaching, one teacher shared a student's comment: "I know when I ask you a question that you are only going to ask me a question in response. But, sometimes the question helps me figure out the next step I need to take. I like that."

Differentiating with Leveled Problems

There are four main ways that teachers can differentiate: by content, by process, by product, and by learning environment. Differentiation by content involves varying the material that is presented to students. Differentiation by process occurs when a teacher delivers instruction to students in different ways. Differentiation by product asks students to present their work in different ways. Offering different learning environments, such as small group settings, is another method of differentiation. Students' learning styles, readiness levels, and interests determine which differentiation strategies are implemented. The leveled problems in this book vary aspects of mathematics problems so that students at various readiness levels can succeed. Mini-lessons include problems at three levels and ideas for differentiation. These are designated by the following symbols:

◯   lower-level challenge

▢   on-level challenge

△   above-level challenge

☆   English language learner support

Ideally, students solve problems that are at just the right level of challenge—beyond what would be too easy, but not so difficult as to cause extreme frustration (Sylwester 2003; Tomlinson 2003; Vygotsky 1986). The goal is to avoid both a lack of challenge, which might leave students bored, as well as too much of a challenge, which might lead to significant anxiety.

There are a variety of ways to level problems. In this book problems are leveled based on the concepts and skills required to find the solution. Problems are leveled by adjusting one or more of the following factors:

Complexity of the Mathematical Language

The mathematical language used in problems can have a significant impact on their level of challenge. For example, the term *more* is easier for students to understand than the term *less*. So a problem that states that there are *more than 7* is simpler to understand than one stating that there are *less than 12*. An even more complex phrase would be *at least 7*.

Complexity of the Task

There are various ways to change the complexity of the task. One example would be the number of solutions that students are expected to identify. Finding one solution that satisfies problem conditions is less challenging than finding more than one solution, which is even less difficult than identifying *all* possible solutions. Similarly, increases and decreases in the number of conditions that must be met and the number of steps that must be completed change the complexity of a problem.

Differentiating with Leveled Problems *(cont.)*

Changing the Numbers

Sometimes it is the size of the numbers that is changed to increase the level of mathematical skills required. A problem may be more complex when it involves three-digit numbers rather than two-digit numbers. Sometimes changes to the "friendliness" of the numbers are made to adapt the difficulty level. For example, if two problems involve basic facts, the one with a sum of 10 is simpler, as sums to ten are emphasized in the curriculum and are more likely to be familiar to students.

Amount of Support

Some problems provide more support for learners than others. Providing a graphic organizer or a table that is partially completed is one way to provide added support for students. Offering information with pictures rather than words can also vary the level of support. The inclusion of such supports often helps students to better understand problems and may offer insights on how to proceed. The exclusion of supports allows a learner to take more responsibility for finding a solution, and it may make the task appear more abstract or challenging.

Differentiation Strategies for English Language Learners

Many English language learners may work at a high readiness level in many mathematical concepts, but may need support in accessing the language content. Specific suggestions for differentiating for English language learners can be found in the *Differentiate* section of some of the mini-lessons. Additionally, the strategies below may assist teachers in differentiating for English language learners.

- Allow students to draw pictures or provide oral responses as an alternative to written responses.
- Pose questions with question stems or frames. Example question stems/frames include:
  - *What would happen if…?*,
  - *Why do you think…?*,
  - *How would you prove…?*,
  - *How is _____ related to _____?*, and
  - *Why is _____ important?*
- Use visuals to give context to questions. Add pictures or icons next to key words, or use realia to help students understand the scenario of the problem.
- Provide sentence stems or frames to help students articulate their thoughts. Sentence stems include:
  - *This is important because…*,
  - *This is similar because…*, and
  - *This is different because…*,

  Sentence frames include:
  - *I agree with _____ because…*,
  - *I disagree with _____ because…*, and
  - *I think _____ because….*
- Partner English language learners with language-proficient students.

Management and Assessment

Organization of the Mini-Lessons

The mini-lessons in this book are organized according to the domains identified in the *Common Core State Standards*, which have also been endorsed by the National Council of Teachers of Mathematics. At grade 1, these domains are *Operations and Algebraic Thinking, Number and Operations in Base-Ten, Measurement and Data,* and *Geometry.* Though organized in this manner, the mini-lessons are independent of one another and may be taught in any order within a domain or among the domains. What is most important is that the lessons are implemented in the order that best fits a teacher's curriculum and practice.

Ways to Use the Mini-Lessons

There are a variety of ways to assign and use the mini-lessons, and they may be implemented in different ways throughout the year. The lessons can provide practice with new concepts or be used to maintain skills previously learned. The problems can be incorporated into a teacher's mathematics lessons once or twice each week, or they may be used to introduce extended or additional instructional periods. They can be used in the regular classroom with the whole class or in small groups. They can also be used to support Response to Intervention (RTI) and after-school programs.

It is important to remember that a student's ability to solve problems depends greatly on the specific content involved and may change over the course of the school year. Establish the expectation that problem assignment is flexible; sometimes students will be assigned to one level (circle, square, or triangle) and sometimes to another. On occasion, you may also wish to allow students to choose their own problems. Much can be learned from students' choices!

Students can also be assigned one, two, or all three of the problems to solve. Although leveled, some students who are capable of wrestling with complex problems need the opportunity to warm up first to build their confidence. Starting at a lower level serves these students well. Teachers may also find that students correctly assigned to a below- or on-level problem will be able to consider a problem at a higher level after solving one of the lower problems. Students can also revisit these problems, investigating those at the higher levels not previously explored.

Grouping Students to Solve Leveled Problems

A differentiated classroom often groups students in a variety of ways, based on the instructional goals of an activity or the tasks students must complete. At times, students may work in heterogeneous groups or pairs with students of varying readiness levels. Other activities may lend themselves to homogeneous groups or pairs of students who share similar readiness levels. Since the problems presented in this book provide below-level, on-level, and above-level challenges, you may wish to partner or group students with others who are working at the same readiness level.

Since students' readiness levels may vary for different mathematical concepts and change throughout a course of study, students may be assigned different levels of problems at different times throughout the year (or even throughout a week). It is important that the grouping of students for solving leveled

Management and Assessment *(cont.)*

Grouping Students to Solve Leveled Problems *(cont.)*

problems stay flexible. Struggling students who feel that they are constantly assigned to work with a certain partner or group may develop feelings of shame or stigma. Above-level students who are routinely assigned to the same group may become disinterested and cause behavior problems. Varying students' groups can help keep the activities interesting and engaging.

Assessment for Learning

In recent years, increased attention has been given to summative assessment in schools. Significantly more instructional time is taken with weekly quizzes, chapter tests, and state-mandated assessments. These tests, although seen as tedious by many, provide information and reports about achievement to students, parents, administrators, and other interested stakeholders. However these summative assessments often do not have a real impact on an individual student's learning. In fact, when teachers return quizzes and tests, many students look at the grade and if it is "good," they bring the assessment home. If it is not an acceptable grade, they often just throw away the assessment.

Research shows that to have an impact on student learning we should rely on assessments *for* learning, rather than assessments *of* learning. That is, we should focus on assessment data we collect during the learning process, not after the instructional cycle is completed. These assessments for learning, or formative assessments, are shown to have the greatest positive impact on student achievement (National Mathematics Advisory Panel 2008). Assessment for learning is an ongoing process that includes a variety of strategies and protocols to inform the progression of student learning.

One might ask, "So, what is the big difference? Don't all assessments accomplish the same goal?" The answer to those key questions is *no*. A great difference is the fact that formative assessment is designed to make student thinking visible. This is a real transformation for many teachers because when the emphasis is on student thinking and reasoning, the focus shifts from whether the answer is correct or incorrect to how the students grapple with a problem. Making student thinking visible entails a change in the manner in which teachers interact with their students. For instance, instead of relying solely on students' written work, teachers gather information through observation, questioning, and listening to their students discuss strategies, justify their reasoning, and explain why they chose to make particular decisions or use a specific representation. Since observations happen in real time, teachers can react in the moment by making an appropriate instructional decision, which may mean asking a well-posed question or suggesting a different model to represent the problem at hand.

Students are often asked to explain what they were thinking as they completed a procedure. Their response is often a recitation of the steps that were used. Such an explanation does not shed any light on whether a student understands the procedure, why it works, or if it will always work. Nor does it provide teachers with any insight into whether a student has a superficial or a deep understanding of the mathematics involved. If, however, students are encouraged to explain their thought processes, teachers will be able to discern the level of their understanding. The vocabulary students use (or do not use) and the confidence with which they are able to answer probing questions can also provide insight into their levels of comprehension.

Management and Assessment *(cont.)*

Assessment for Learning *(cont.)*

One of the most important features of formative assessment is that it actively involves students in their own learning. In assessment for learning, students are asked to reflect on their own work. They may be asked to consider multiple representations of a problem and then decide which of those representations makes the most sense, or which is the most efficient, or how they relate to one another. Students may be asked to make conjectures and then prove or disprove them by negation or counterexamples. Notice that it is the students doing the hard work of making decisions and thinking through the mathematical processes. Students who work at this level of mathematics, regardless of their grade level, demonstrate a deep understanding of mathematical concepts.

Assessment for learning makes learning a shared endeavor between teachers and students. In effective learning environments students take responsibility for their learning and feel safe taking risks, and teachers have opportunities to gain a deeper understanding of what their students know and are able to do. Implementing a variety of tools and protocols when assessing for learning can help the process become seamless. Some specific formative assessment tools and protocols include:

- Student Response Forms or Journals
- Range Questions
- Gallery Walks
- Observation Protocols
- Feedback
- Exit Cards

Student Response Forms or Journals

Providing students with an organized workspace for the problems they solve can help a teacher to better understand a student's thinking and more easily identify misconceptions. Students often think that recording an answer is enough. If students do include further details, they often only write enough to fill the limited space that might be provided on an activity sheet. To promote the expectation that students show all of their work and record more of their thinking, use the included *Student Response Form* (page 130; studentresponse.pdf), or have students use a designated journal or notebook for solving problems. The prompts on the *Student Response Form* and the additional space provided encourage students to offer more details.

Range Questions

Range questions allow for a variety of responses and teachers can use them to quickly gain access to students' understanding. Range questions are included in the activate section of many mini-lessons. The questions or problems that are posed are designed to provide insight into the spectrum of understanding that your students bring to the day's problems. For instance, you might ask *What does it mean to have groups that are* equal *in number? When might we want to be sure that groups have the same number of people?* The level of sophistication in the responses varies and can help you decide which students to assign to which of the leveled problems.

Management and Assessment *(cont.)*

Gallery Walks

Gallery walks can be used in many ways, but they all promote the sharing of students' problem-solving strategies and solutions. Pairs or small groups of students can record their pictures, tables, graphs, diagrams, computational procedures, and justifications on chart paper that they hang in designated areas of the classroom prior to the debriefing component of the lesson. Or, simply have students place their *Student Response Forms* at their workspaces and have students take a tour of their classmates' thinking. Though suggested occasionally for specific mini-lessons, this strategy can be included with any of the mini-lessons.

Observation Protocols

Observation protocols facilitate the data gathering that teachers must do as they document evidence of student learning. Assessment of learning is a key component in a teacher's ability to say, "I know that my students can apply these mathematical ideas because I have this evidence." Some important learning behaviors for teachers to focus on include: level of engagement in the problem/task; incorporation of multiple representations; inclusion of appropriate labels in pictures, tables, graphs, and solutions; use of accountable talk; inclusion of reflection on their work; and connections made between and among other mathematical ideas, previous problems, and their own life experiences. There is no one right form, nor could all of these areas be included on a form while leaving room for comments. Protocols should be flexible and allow you to identify categories of learning important to you and your students. Two observation forms are provided in the appendices—one can be used with individual students (page 131; individualobs.pdf), and one can be used when observing a group (page 132; groupobs.pdf).

Feedback

Feedback is a critical component of formative assessment. Teachers who do not give letter grades on projects, quizzes, or tests, but who provide either neutral feedback or inquisitive feedback, find their students take a greater interest in the work they receive back than they did when their papers were graded. There are different types of feedback, but effective feedback focuses on the evidence in student work. Many students respond favorably to an "assessment sandwich." The first comment might be a positive comment or praise for something well done, followed by a critical question or request for further clarification, followed by another neutral or positive comment.

Exit Cards

Exit cards are an effective way of assessing students' thinking at the end of a lesson in preparation for future instruction. There are multiple ways in which exit cards can be used. A similar problem to the one students have previously solved can be posed, or students can be asked to identify topics of confusion, what they liked best, or what they think they learned from a lesson. One simple exit card task involves distributing cards that show three thumbs: one pointing up, one pointing horizontally, and one pointing down (exitcard.pdf). Students readily pick the one that they think best reflects their understanding of the lesson and place the cards into a receptacle. As one student said as she dropped her card in the box, "This has been a great thumbs-up problem-solving day!" Exit-card tasks are suggested in the *Differentiate* sections of some of the mini-lessons, but they may be added to any mini-lesson.

How to Use This Book

Mini-Lesson Plan

Lessons are organized by **Common Core State Standards** domains.

Suggested **Problem-Solving Strategies** outline strategies students may want to use in solving the problem. However, these are not the only strategies that can be used to solve the problem.

The McREL mathematics **Standards** for each lesson are provided.

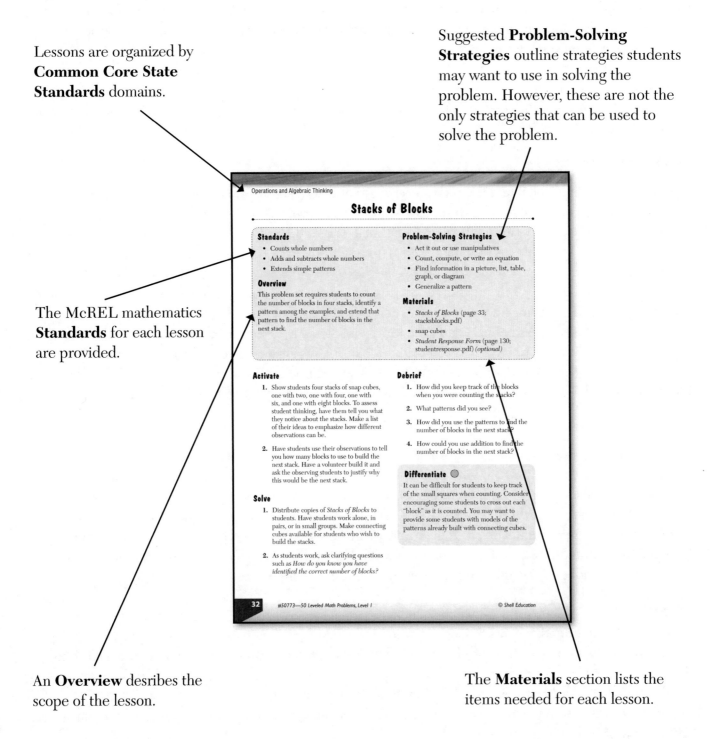

Operations and Algebraic Thinking

Stacks of Blocks

Standards
- Counts whole numbers
- Adds and subtracts whole numbers
- Extends simple patterns

Overview
This problem set requires students to count the number of blocks in four stacks, identify a pattern among the examples, and extend that pattern to find the number of blocks in the next stack.

Problem-Solving Strategies
- Act it out or use manipulatives
- Count, compute, or write an equation
- Find information in a picture, list, table, graph, or diagram
- Generalize a pattern

Materials
- *Stacks of Blocks* (page 33; stacksblocks.pdf)
- snap cubes
- *Student Response Form* (page 130; studentresponse.pdf) *(optional)*

Activate
1. Show students four stacks of snap cubes, one with two, one with four, one with six, and one with eight blocks. To assess student thinking, have them tell you what they notice about the stacks. Make a list of their ideas to emphasize how different observations can be.

2. Have students use their observations to tell you how many blocks to use to build the next stack. Have a volunteer build it and ask the observing students to justify why this would be the next stack.

Solve
1. Distribute copies of *Stacks of Blocks* to students. Have students work alone, in pairs, or in small groups. Make connecting cubes available for students who wish to build the stacks.

2. As students work, ask clarifying questions such as *How do you know you have identified the correct number of blocks?*

Debrief
1. How did you keep track of the blocks when you were counting the stacks?

2. What patterns did you see?

3. How did you use the patterns to find the number of blocks in the next stack?

4. How could you use addition to find the number of blocks in the next stack?

Differentiate ◯
It can be difficult for students to keep track of the small squares when counting. Consider encouraging some students to cross out each "block" as it is counted. You may want to provide some students with models of the patterns already built with connecting cubes.

32   #50773—50 Leveled Math Problems, Level 1   © Shell Education

The McREL mathematics **Standards** for each lesson are provided.

An **Overview** describes the scope of the lesson.

The **Materials** section lists the items needed for each lesson.

How to Use This Book *(cont.)*

Mini-Lesson Plan *(cont.)*

The **Activate** section suggests how you can access or assess students' prior knowledge. This section might recommend ways to have students review vocabulary, recall experiences related to the problem contexts, remember relevant mathematical ideas, or solve simpler related problems.

The **Debrief** section provides questions designed to deepen students' understanding of the mathematics and the problem-solving process. Because the leveled problems share common features, it is possible to debrief either with small groups or as a whole class.

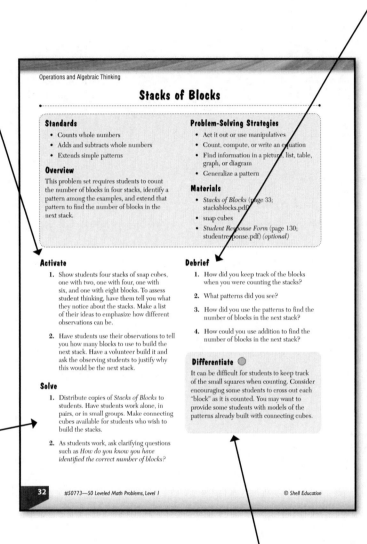

Operations and Algebraic Thinking

Stacks of Blocks

Standards
- Counts whole numbers
- Adds and subtracts whole numbers
- Extends simple patterns

Overview
This problem set requires students to count the number of blocks in four stacks, identify a pattern among the examples, and extend that pattern to find the number of blocks in the next stack.

Problem-Solving Strategies
- Act it out or use manipulatives
- Count, compute, or write an equation
- Find information in a picture, list, table, graph, or diagram
- Generalize a pattern

Materials
- *Stacks of Blocks* (page 33; stacksblocks.pdf)
- snap cubes
- *Student Response Form* (page 130; studentresponse.pdf) *(optional)*

Activate
1. Show students four stacks of snap cubes, one with two, one with four, one with six, and one with eight blocks. To assess student thinking, have them tell you what they notice about the stacks. Make a list of their ideas to emphasize how different observations can be.

2. Have students use their observations to tell you how many blocks to use to build the next stack. Have a volunteer build it and ask the observing students to justify why this would be the next stack.

Solve
1. Distribute copies of *Stacks of Blocks* to students. Have students work alone, in pairs, or in small groups. Make connecting cubes available for students who wish to build the stacks.

2. As students work, ask clarifying questions such as *How do you know you have identified the correct number of blocks?*

Debrief
1. How did you keep track of the blocks when you were counting the stacks?

2. What patterns did you see?

3. How did you use the patterns to find the number of blocks in the next stack?

4. How could you use addition to find the number of blocks in the next stack?

Differentiate ○
It can be difficult for students to keep track of the small squares when counting. Consider encouraging some students to cross out each "block" as it is counted. You may want to provide some students with models of the patterns already built with connecting cubes.

32   #50773—50 Leveled Math Problems, Level 1   © Shell Education

The **Solve** section provides suggestions on how to group students for the problem they will solve. It also provides questions to ask, observations to make, or procedures to follow to guide students in their work.

The **Differentiate** section includes additional suggestions to meet the unique needs of students. This section may offer support for English language learners, scaffolding for below-level students, or enrichment opportunities for above-level students. The following symbols are used to indicate appropriate readiness levels for the provided differentiation:

○ below level

□ on level

△ above level

☆ English language learner

How to Use This Book *(cont.)*

Lesson Resources

Leveled Problems

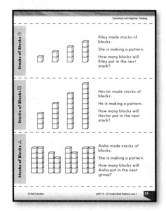

Each activity sheet offers **leveled problems** at three levels of challenge—below level, on level, and above level. Cut the activity sheet apart and distribute the appropriate problem to each student, or present all of the leveled problems on an activity sheet to every student.

Record-Keeping Chart

Use the **Record-Keeping Chart** (page 133) to keep track of the problems each student completes.

Observation Forms

Use the **Individual Observation Form** (page 131) to document students' progress as they work through problems on their own. Use the **Group Observation Form** (page 132) to keep a record of students' success in working with their peers to solve problems.

Teacher Resource CD

Helpful reproducibles are provided on the accompanying **Teacher Resource CD**. A detailed listing of the CD contents can be found on pages 140–142. The CD includes:

- Resources to support the implementation of the mini-lessons
- Manipulative templates
- Reproducible PDFs of all leveled problems and assessment tools
- Correlations to standards

How to Use This Book (cont.)

Lesson Resources (cont.)

Student Response Form

Students can attach their leveled problem to the form.

Students have space to show their work, provide their solution, and explain their thinking.

Appendix A

Name: _____ Date: _____

Student Response Form

Problem:

(glue your problem here)

My Work and Illustrations: *(picture, table, list, graph)* | **My Solution:**

My Explanation:

_____

_____

Correlations to Standards

Shell Education is committed to producing educational materials that are research- and standards-based. In this effort, we have correlated all of our products to the academic standards of all 50 United States, the District of Columbia, the Department of Defense Dependent Schools, and all Canadian provinces. We have also correlated to the *Common Core State Standards*.

How To Find Standards Correlations

To print a customized correlation report of this product for your state, visit our website at **http://www.shelleducation.com** and follow the on-screen directions. If you require assistance in printing correlation reports, please contact Customer Service at 1-877-777-3450.

Purpose and Intent of Standards

Legislation mandates that all states adopt academic standards that identify the skills students will learn in kindergarten through grade twelve. Many states also have standards for Pre-K. This same legislation sets requirements to ensure the standards are detailed and comprehensive.

Standards are designed to focus instruction and guide adoption of curricula. Standards are statements that describe the criteria necessary for students to meet specific academic goals. They define the knowledge, skills, and content students should acquire at each level. Standards are also used to develop standardized tests to evaluate students' academic progress. Teachers are required to demonstrate how their lessons meet state standards. State standards are used in the development of all of our products, so educators can be assured they meet the academic requirements of each state.

McREL Compendium

We use the Mid-continent Research for Education and Learning (McREL) Compendium to create standards correlations. Each year, McREL analyzes state standards and revises the compendium. By following this procedure, McREL is able to produce a general compilation of national standards. Each lesson in this product is based on one or more McREL standards, which are located on the Teacher Resource CD (mcrel.pdf).

TESOL Standards

The lessons in this book promote English language development for English language learners. The standards listed on the Teacher Resource CD (tesol.pdf) support the language objectives presented throughout the lessons.

Common Core State Standards

The lessons in this book are aligned to the Common Core State Standards (CCSS). The standards listed on pages 27–29 (ccss.pdf) support the objectives presented throughout the lessons.

NCTM Standards

The lessons in this book are aligned to the National Council of Teachers of Mathematics (NCTM) standards. The standards listed on the Teacher Resource CD (nctm.pdf) support the objectives presented throughout the lessons.

Correlations to Standards *(cont.)*

Common Core State Standards Correlation

Common Core Standard	Lesson
1.OA.1 Use addition and subtraction within 20 to solve word problems involving situations of adding to, taking from, putting together, taking apart, and comparing, with unknowns in all positions, e.g., by using objects, drawings, and equations with a symbol for the unknown number to represent the problem.	At the Farm, page 30; Stacks of Blocks, page 32; Draw and Count, page 34; Lots of Apples, page 36; From the Garden, page 40; Smiley Cupcakes, page 42; A Day at the Beach, page 44; At the Party Store, page 48; Get a Prize, page 50; Toss It, page 56; Ask a Question, page 60; How Many Animals?, page 62; How Many Pennies?, page 64; Finding Favorites, page 104; Make a Graph, page 106; Point Totals, page 108; What Do We Know?, page 110
1.OA.2 Solve word problems that call for addition of three whole numbers whose sum is less than or equal to 20, e.g., by using objects, drawings, and equations with a symbol for the unknown number to represent the problem.	At the Farm, page 30; Draw and Count, page 34; Smiley Cupcakes, page 42; Get a Prize, page 50
1.OA.4 Understand subtraction as an unknown-addend problem.	At the Party Store, page 48
1.OA.5 Relate counting to addition and subtraction (e.g., by counting on 2 to add 2).	At the Farm, page 30; Stacks of Blocks, page 32; Draw and Count, page 34; Lots of Apples, page 36; From the Garden, page 40; On the Line, page 52; Where Did You Start?, page 58; Ask a Question, page 60; How Many Pennies?, page 64; Hands, Toes, and Legs, page 66; Finding Favorites, page 104; Make a Graph, page 106; Point Totals, page 108; What Do We Know?, page 110
1.OA.6 Add and subtract within 20, demonstrating fluency for addition and subtraction within 10. Use strategies such as counting on; making ten (e.g., $8 + 6 = 8 + 2 + 4 = 10 + 4 = 14$); decomposing a number leading to a ten (e.g., $13 - 4 = 13 - 3 - 1 = 10 - 1 = 9$); using the relationship between addition and subtraction (e.g., knowing that $8 + 4 = 12$, one knows $12 - 8 = 4$); and creating equivalent but easier or known sums (e.g., adding $6 + 7$ by creating the known equivalent $6 + 6 + 1 = 12 + 1 = 13$).	At the Farm, page 30; Draw and Count, page 34; Lots of Apples, page 36; From the Garden, page 40; Smiley Cupcakes, page 42; A Day at the Beach, page 44; At the Party Store, page 48; Get a Prize, page 50; Which Numbers?, page 54; Toss It, page 56; Where Did You Start?, page 58; Ask a Question, page 60; How Many Animals?, page 62; How Many Pennies?, page 64; Finding Favorites, page 104; Point Totals, page 108; What Do We Know?, page 110; Build a Design, page 118

Operations and Algebraic Thinking

Correlations to Standards (cont.)

Common Core State Standards Correlation (cont.)

Common Core Standard	Lesson
1.OA.7 Understand the meaning of the equal sign, and determine if equations involving addition and subtraction are true or false. For example, which of the following equations are true and which are false? 6 = 6, 7 = 8 – 1, 5 + 2 = 2 + 5, 4 + 1 = 5 + 2.	Make It Equal, page 38; Figure It, page 46; Which Numbers?, page 54
1.OA.8 Determine the unknown whole number in an addition or subtraction equation relating three whole numbers.	Lots of Apples, page 36; A Day at the Beach, page 44; Figure It, page 46; Which Numbers?, page 54; Where Did You Start?, page 58
1.NBT.1 Count to 120, starting at any number less than 120. In this range, read and write numerals and represent a number of objects with a written numeral.	At the Farm, page 30; Stacks of Blocks, page 32; Draw and Count, page 34; Make It Equal, page 38; From the Garden, page 40; Tile Patterns, page 72; Finding Favorites, page 104; Make a Graph, page 106; Point Totals, page 108; What Do We Know?, page 110; First Names, page 112
1.NBT.2 Understand that the two digits of a two-digit number represent amounts of tens and ones. Understand the following as special cases: • 10 can be thought of as a bundle of ten ones—called a "ten." • The numbers from 11 to 19 are composed of a ten and one, two, three, four, five, six, seven, eight, or nine ones. • The numbers 10, 20, 30, 40, 50, 60, 70, 80, 90 refer to one, two, three, four, five, six, seven, eight, or nine tens (and 0 ones).	Show It, page 68; More or Less, page 74; T-Shirt Numbers, page 80; Ring Toss, page 86; What is the Number?, page 90
1.NBT.3 Compare two two-digit numbers based on meanings of the tens and ones digits, recording the results of comparisons with the symbols >, =, and <.	More or Less, page 74; T-Shirt Numbers, page 80; June Birthdays, page 82; What is the Number?, page 90; Number Groups, page 92
1.NBT.4 Add within 100, including adding a two-digit number and a one-digit number, and adding a two-digit number and a multiple of 10, using concrete models or drawings and strategies based on place value, properties of operations, and/or the relationship between addition and subtraction; relate the strategy to a written method and explain the reasoning used. Understand that in adding two-digit numbers, one adds tens and tens, ones and ones; and sometimes it is necessary to compose a ten.	Sticker Stories, page 70; What Did You Buy?, page 84; Ring Toss, page 86; Favorite Numbers, page 88

Operations and Algebraic Thinking (cont.) / *Number and Operations in Base Ten*

Correlations to Standards *(cont.)*

Common Core State Standards Correlation *(cont.)*

	Common Core Standard	Lesson
Number and Operations in Base Ten *(cont.)*	**1.NBT.5** Given a two-digit number, mentally find 10 more or 10 less than the number, without having to count; explain the reasoning used.	Shrinking Machines, page 76
	1.NBT.6 Subtract multiples of 10 in the range 10–90 from multiples of 10 in the range 10–90 (positive or zero differences), using concrete models or drawings and strategies based on place value, properties of operations, and/or the relationship between addition and subtraction; relate the strategy to a written method and explain the reasoning used.	Sticker Stories, page 70
Measurement and Data	**1.MD.1** Order three objects by length; compare the lengths of two objects indirectly by using a third object.	How Long?, page 94
	1.MD.2 Express the length of an object as a whole number of length units, by laying multiple copies of a shorter object (the length unit) end to end; understand that the length measurement of an object is the number of same-size length units that span it with no gaps or overlaps.	Find It, page 96; Rod Lengths, page 98
	1.MD.3 Tell and write time in hours and half-hours using analog and digital clocks.	What Time?, page 100; What Happens?, page 102
	1.MD.4 Organize, represent, and interpret data with up to three categories; ask and answer questions about the total number of data points, how many in each category, and how many more or less are in one category than in another.	Finding Favorites, page 104; Make a Graph, page 106; Point Totals, page 108; What Do We Know?, page 110; First Names, page 112
Geometry	**1.G.1** Distinguish between defining attributes (e.g., triangles are closed and three-sided) versus non-defining attributes (e.g., color, orientation, overall size); build and draw shapes to possess defining attributes.	What Shape Is Next?, page 114; What Shape Am I?, page 116; Shape Creatures, page 124; Venn Diagram, page 126
	1.G.2 Compose two-dimensional shapes (rectangles, squares, trapezoids, triangles, half-circles, and quarter-circles) or three-dimensional shapes (cubes, right rectangular prisms, right circular cones, and right circular cylinders) to create a composite shape, and compose new shapes from the composite shape.	Build a Design, page 118; Make It, page 120; What Comes Next?, page 122
	1.G.3 Partition circles and rectangles into two and four equal shares, describe the shares using the words *halves, fourths,* and *quarters,* and use the phrases *half of, fourth of,* and *quarter of.* Describe the whole as two of, or four of the shares. Understand for these examples that decomposing into more equal shares creates smaller shares.	Tasty Treats, page 128

At the Farm

Standards

- Counts whole numbers
- Solves real-world problems involving addition and subtraction of whole numbers

Overview

Students are shown a group of countable animals and read about another set of these animals that they cannot see. The task is to find the total number of animals.

Problem-Solving Strategies

- Count, compute, or write an equation
- Find information in a picture, list, table, graph, or diagram
- Organize information in a picture, list, table, graph, or diagram

Materials

- *At the Farm* (page 31; atfarm.pdf)
- counters
- *Student Response Form* (page 130; studentresponse.pdf) *(optional)*

Activate

1. Display four counters for students. Have them count to determine how many there are. Take two more counters and place them out of sight in a closed fist or pocket. Tell students the number of counters they cannot see and ask how many counters there are in all.

2. Have counters available to students as well as paper and pencils. Tell students that they can work in pairs or alone to find the number of counters. As the students work, observe their strategies. You may want to note which students use the counters, make a drawing, count on their fingers, count on from four, count all, use mental arithmetic, or write an equation.

3. Have students share their strategies. Encourage a variety of explanations. Refer to your observations to make sure each technique used is shared.

Solve

1. Distribute copies of *At the Farm* to students. Have students work alone, in pairs, or in small groups.

2. Observe students in the same ways as suggested in Step 2 of the *Activate* section.

Debrief

1. How did you find the number of animals?

2. What is another way to find this answer?

3. If there were one more animal that you could not see, how many would there be in all?

Differentiate

Many students may represent the second set of animals and then count all of the animals rather than counting on from one of the sets. Pairing such students with those who do count on will expose them to a different way of thinking. Nearly all students do eventually count on, though they may return to counting all when greater numbers are first introduced.

At the Farm ○

There are 2 horses inside the barn.

How many horses are there in all?

At the Farm □

There are 3 chickens behind the rock.

How many chickens are there in all?

At the Farm △

There are 2 pigs behind the tractor.

There are 3 pigs behind the fence.

How many pigs are there in all?

Stacks of Blocks

Standards
- Counts whole numbers
- Adds and subtracts whole numbers
- Extends simple patterns

Overview
This problem set requires students to count the number of blocks in four stacks, identify a pattern among the examples, and extend that pattern to find the number of blocks in the next stack.

Problem-Solving Strategies
- Act it out or use manipulatives
- Count, compute, or write an equation
- Find information in a picture, list, table, graph, or diagram
- Generalize a pattern

Materials
- *Stacks of Blocks* (page 33; stacksblocks.pdf)
- snap cubes
- *Student Response Form* (page 130; studentresponse.pdf) *(optional)*

Activate
1. Show students four stacks of snap cubes, one with two, one with four, one with six, and one with eight blocks. To assess student thinking, have them tell you what they notice about the stacks. Make a list of their ideas to emphasize how different observations can be.

2. Have students use their observations to tell you how many blocks to use to build the next stack. Have a volunteer build it and ask the observing students to justify why this would be the next stack.

Solve
1. Distribute copies of *Stacks of Blocks* to students. Have students work alone, in pairs, or in small groups. Make connecting cubes available for students who wish to build the stacks.

2. As students work, ask clarifying questions such as *How do you know you have identified the correct number of blocks?*

Debrief
1. How did you keep track of the blocks when you were counting the stacks?

2. What patterns did you see?

3. How did you use the patterns to find the number of blocks in the next stack?

4. How could you use addition to find the number of blocks in the next stack?

Differentiate
It can be difficult for students to keep track of the small squares when counting. Consider encouraging some students to cross out each "block" as it is counted. You may want to provide some students with models of the patterns already built with connecting cubes.

Stacks of Blocks ◯

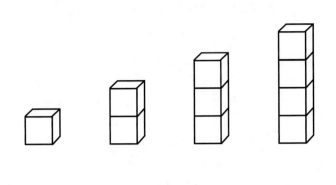

Riley made stacks of blocks.

She is making a pattern.

How many blocks will Riley put in the next stack?

Stacks of Blocks ▢

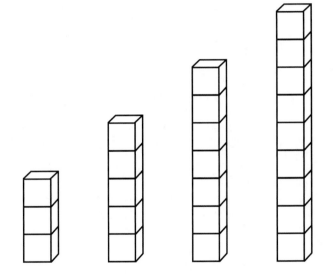

Hector made stacks of blocks.

He is making a pattern.

How many blocks will Hector put in the next stack?

Stacks of Blocks ◁

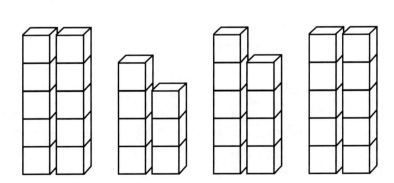

Aisha made stacks of blocks.

She is making a pattern.

How many blocks will Aisha put in the next group?

Draw and Count

Standards

- Counts whole numbers
- Adds and subtracts whole numbers

Overview

In these problems students are asked to draw and count the total number of stars.

Problem-Solving Strategies

- Count, compute, or write an equation
- Organize information in a picture, list, table, graph, or diagram
- Guess and check or make an estimate

Materials

- *Draw and Count* (page 35; drawcount.pdf)
- small star stickers or stamps (*optional*)
- *Student Response Form* (page 130; studentresponse.pdf) (*optional*)

Activate

1. Draw a circle and a square. Have the students watch you draw six stars in the circle and two stars in the square. Count aloud as you draw the stars and when drawn, recount them to check.

2. Tell students to watch you closely as you count all of the stars and then proceed to do so incorrectly. The first time skip two of the stars. Ask if anyone got a different answer. The next time count one of the stars twice. Again, ask if anyone got a different answer. Ask students to tell you what you did wrong. Talk about the errors with students. Then have a volunteer count the stars correctly.

3. To assess students' thinking ask *What might you do to help you count and solve problems accurately?*

Solve

1. Distribute copies of *Draw and Count* to students. Have students work alone, in pairs, or in small groups.

Debrief

1. What did you do to make sure that you counted correctly?

2. How many stars did you draw in each shape to get the total number of stars? How did you find your answer?

3. Can someone show us his or her drawing and tell us why it is correct?

4. Did anyone get a different answer they can share with us?

5. Can there be more than one answer to a problem?

Differentiate ◯ ◻ △ ☆

Students who struggle with fine motor skills may benefit from using stickers or stamping tools. The use of these tools may also motivate other students, so make them available to the whole group. You may wish to offer an exit card task such as the following: *Draw 5 stars. Draw 4 more stars. How many stars did you draw in all?*

Draw and Count ○

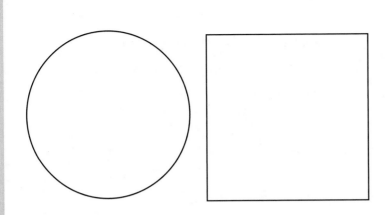

Draw 3 ☆ in the ○.

Draw 4 ☆ in the ⬜.

How many ☆ did you draw in all?

Draw and Count ⬜

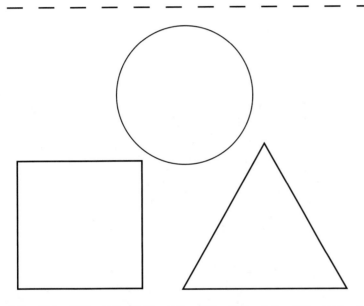

Draw 2 ☆ in the ○.

Draw 5 ☆ in the ⬜.

Draw ☆ in the △ so that there are 10 ☆ in all.

How many ☆ did you draw in the △?

Draw and Count △

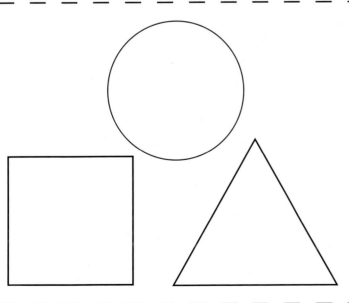

Draw 3 ☆ in the △.

Draw more ☆ in the ⬜ than the ○.

Draw 15 ☆ in all.

How many ☆ did you draw in the ⬜?

Lots of Apples

Standard

Solves real-world problems involving addition and subtraction of whole numbers

Overview

In this problem set students draw tally marks to represent apples and then use their drawings to find the answers to questions posed.

Problem-Solving Strategies

- Count, compute, or write an equation
- Organize information in a picture, list, table, graph, or diagram

Materials

- *Lots of Apples* (page 37; lotsapples.pdf)
- *Student Response Form* (page 130; studentresponse.pdf) *(optional)*

Activate

1. Ask students what tally marks are. Ask a volunteer to make tally marks on the board to show the number six. Ask *If we were representing six flowers, why might we use tally marks instead of drawing flowers?*

2. Display the problem below for students. Have them solve it and write the corresponding equation.

   I have 1 apple.

   I buy 4 more apples.

   How many apples do I have now?

3. Edit the problem by replacing the number 4 with the word *some*, and changing the last line to *I have 5 apples.* Ask students what equation they would write now.

Solve

1. Distribute copies of *Lots of Apples* to students. Point out the expectation that students write equations. Have students work alone, in pairs, or in small groups.

2. Encourage extended thinking by asking questions such as *How else might you solve it?*

Debrief

1. Who made a drawing representing the apples?

2. How did making a drawing help you?

3. How can drawings show us how you solved a problem?

Differentiate ⬤ ■ △ ☆

Some students may draw tally marks so close together that they are difficult to count. Drawing circles may be easier for these students. Others may have difficulty with one-to-one correspondence when they count objects, regardless of what is drawn. You may want these students to work with a partner who can observe the accuracy of their counting process. You may also want to demonstrate the common practice of grouping tally marks in sets of five.

Lots of Apples

Lisa has 5 🍎 . Diego has 2 🍎 .

Make a tally mark for each 🍎 .

Lisa:

Diego:

How many 🍎 do Lisa and Diego have in all?

Write an addition equation for this problem.

Lots of Apples

Jin has 6 🍎 . Meg has 4 more 🍎 than Jin has.

Make a tally mark for each 🍎 .

Jin:

Meg:

How many 🍎 does Meg have?

Write an addition equation for this problem.

Lots of Apples

Dan has 3 🍎 . Then Ali gives him some more 🍎 .

Now Dan has 12 🍎 . How many 🍎 did Ali give Dan?

Draw tally marks to show how you know. Write an addition equation for this problem.

Make It Equal

Standards

- Counts whole numbers
- Understands symbolic, concrete, and pictorial representations of numbers

Overview

Students count objects and then determine how to move some of the objects from one set to another so that there is the same amount in each set.

Problem-Solving Strategies

- Act it out or use manipulatives
- Count, compute, or write an equation
- Find information in a picture, list, table, graph, or diagram
- Guess and check or make an estimate

Materials

- *Make It Equal* (page 39; makeequal.pdf)
- counters
- *Student Response Form* (page 130; studentresponse.pdf) *(optional)*

Activate

1. To assess students' understanding of equality ask them what it means to have groups that are equal in number, and when we might want to be sure that groups have the same number of people.

2. Invite three students to stand on one side of the room and five students to stand on the other side.

3. Ask *How can we move students from one group to the other so that there is the same number of students in each group?*

Solve

1. Distribute copies of *Make It Equal* to students. Have students work alone or in pairs. Explain that the goal is to have the same number of ducks in each pond. Make counters available. Be sure students understand that they may only move ducks from one pond to one other pond and and that they will use arrows to show the moves.

2. Ask clarifying questions if you are unsure about the moves students are making.

Debrief

1. How did you decide which ducks to move?

2. How did using the counters help some of you?

3. Why is it important to check the number of ducks in each pool after you move the ducks?

Differentiate ◯ ▢ △ ☆

Some students may solve the problem(s) visually without ever counting the number of ducks in each pond. Others may think about the numbers abstractly to decide how many ducks to move or from which pond to move them. Pairing students with different strengths allows both to contribute and exposes each to a different way of thinking.

Make It Equal ◯

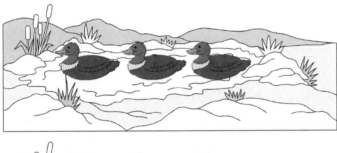

Move ducks so there are the same number in each pond.

Only ducks from one pond may be moved.

Use arrows to show the moves. ↑↓

Make It Equal ▢

Move ducks so there are the same number in each pond.

Only ducks from one pond may be moved.

Use arrows to show the moves. ↑↓

Make It Equal △

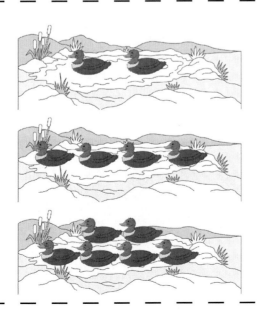

Move ducks so there are the same number in each pond.

Only ducks from one pond may be moved.

Use arrows to show the moves. ↑↓

From the Garden

Standards

- Adds and subtracts whole numbers
- Solves real-world problems involving addition and subtraction of whole numbers

Overview

These problems focus on the taking-apart model of subtraction. In each problem, it is the result that students must find.

Problem-Solving Strategies

- Count, compute, or write an equation
- Find information in a picture, list, table, graph, or diagram

Materials

- *From the Garden* (page 41; fromgarden.pdf)
- *Student Response Form* (page 130; studentresponse.pdf) *(optional)*

Activate

1. Allow students the opportunity to share their experiences with gardening by asking if they have ever picked a fruit or vegetable from a garden.

2. Sketch a picture of several pumpkins and have a student count the number of pumpkins aloud as you point to them one by one. Ask *If you picked two of these pumpkins, how many pumpkins would still be in the garden?*

3. Have students suggest ways to find the answer. Encourage more than one response.

Solve

1. Distribute copies of *From the Garden* to students. Have students work alone, in pairs, or in small groups.

2. Encourage students working with others to each count the items shown to check for accuracy.

Debrief

1. How did you find your answer?

2. How could we find the answer without counting?

3. What equation could we write for this problem?

4. If you were using counting, how could you find the answer if only one tomato plant were shown?

Differentiate ○ ■ △ ☆

Some students cross off items that have been taken away and then do not notice one or more of those marks when they count the number of items that remain. Encourage students to make their marks with a different colored pencil or a crayon to make them more noticeable. Consider the following exit-card task: *I have 10 blueberries. I eat three of them. How many blueberries do I have left?* Have students discuss the situation together and then show their individual work and answers on the cards.

From the Garden

Cassie ate 6 .

How many  are left?

From the Garden

Joshua picked 9 🌷.

How many 🌷 are left?

From the Garden

Mr. Collins picked 5 🍅 from each plant.

How many 🍅 are left?

Smiley Cupcakes

Standards

- Adds and subtracts whole numbers
- Solves real-world problems involving addition and subtraction of whole numbers

Overview

Students find information in pictures and use addition and subtraction skills to solve problems involving boxes of cupcakes.

Problem-Solving Strategies

- Count, compute, or write an equation
- Find information in a picture, list, table, graph, or diagram
- Guess and check or make an estimate

Materials

- *Smiley Cupcakes* (page 43; smileycupcakes.pdf)
- *Student Response Form* (page 130; studentresponse.pdf) (*optional*)

Activate

1. In small groups have students talk about the meanings of the terms *small*, *medium*, and *large*. Encourage them to make sure each member of their group understands these words. Ask a few groups to share their thinking with the class.

2. Ask students where they might use or hear one of these words. Encourage a variety of responses such as when ordering drinks or pizzas, buying T-shirts, or describing an object.

3. Show students the numbers 6, 2, and 4, in that order. Ask *If a cupcake store sold small, medium, and large boxes of cupcakes, which number of cupcakes do you think would be in a small box? Medium? Large?*

Solve

1. Distribute copies of *Smiley Cupcakes* to students. Have students work alone, in pairs, or in small groups. Direct their attention to the top of the page and ask them what the pictures tell them. Then ask *How will this information help you to solve the problems?*

2. Ask clarifying or refocusing questions, such as *What would we see if this box were open? What does this number represent? What are you doing now?*

3. Encourage students with descriptive feedback, such as *I see you have written the number of cupcakes on each box to help you remember how many are inside.*

Debrief

1. How did you find the number of cupcakes?

2. How could we write an equation to find the number of cupcakes in the boxes?

Differentiate ◯

Some students may have difficulty finding their place when looking back and forth between the pictures that show the number of cupcakes in each box and the problems. Encourage these students to write the numbers directly on the boxes in the problems.

Smiley Cupcakes

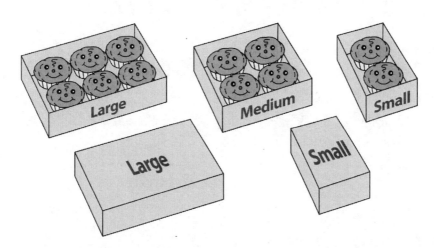

How many cupcakes are there in the closed boxes?

Smiley Cupcakes

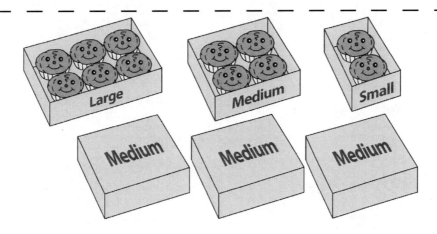

How many cupcakes are there in the closed boxes?

How could you buy this number of cupcakes with two boxes?

Smiley Cupcakes

 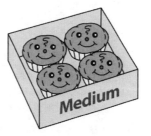 

You want to buy 14 cupcakes, but you only want to buy 3 boxes of cupcakes.

What boxes could you buy? Find another way.

A Day at the Beach

Standards

- Adds and subtracts whole numbers
- Solves real-world problems involving addition and subtraction of whole numbers

Overview

In this problem set students choose from a set of numbers and write missing numbers so that stories make sense.

Problem-Solving Strategies

- Count, compute, or write an equation
- Guess and check or make an estimate
- Use logical reasoning

Materials

- *A Day at the Beach* (page 45; daybeach.pdf)
- *Student Response Form* (page 130; studentresponse.pdf) *(optional)*

Activate

1. Ask students about things that people do at the beach. Allow several students to share responses.

2. Show students the following problem:

   Use each number in the box once to complete the story.

6	10	4

   There are _____ children swimming and _____ children riding waves.

   There are _____ children in all.

   Have students talk with a partner about where the numbers could go in the story so that the story makes sense.

3. Encourage volunteers to share their responses. Make sure students note that the six and four may be placed in either of the first two blanks, while the ten must be placed in the third blank to indicate the total.

Solve

1. Distribute copies of *A Day at the Beach* to students. Have students work alone, in pairs, or in small groups.

2. Ask clarifying or refocusing questions if students appear to struggle with choosing appropriate number placement.

Debrief

1. Who can read the story with the numbers?

2. How did you decide where to write the numbers?

3. Did anyone find a different way to write the numbers so that the story makes sense? Why do you think there is more than one way?

4. What would you have to think about to make a new set of numbers for the story?

Differentiate ◯ ▢ △ ☆

Some students may best detect the relationships among the numbers in the story by focusing on the words and actions. Others may note relationships among the numbers themselves before reading the story. Encourage students to share their different ways of thinking.

A Day at the Beach

Use each number from the box below once so that the story makes sense.

3	5	2

I saw _____ children swimming in the water. I saw _____ children playing in the sand. I saw _____ children in all.

Use each number from the box below once so that the story makes sense.

4	2	1	6

There are _____ shovels and _____ pails on the beach. There are _____ more shovels than pails. There is _____ lifeguard on the beach.

Use each number from the box below once so that the story makes sense.

1	3	10	5

Mason's mother is driving her sons to the beach. Mason has _____ brother. There are _____ people in the car. At the beach the boys each make _____ sand castles. They make _____ sand castles in all.

Figure It

Standards

- Adds and subtracts whole numbers
- Recognizes regularities in a variety of contexts

Overview

This problem set presents equations with shapes as place holders for numbers. Students identify numbers that make the equations true.

Problem-Solving Strategies

- Count, compute, or write an equation
- Guess and check or make an estimate
- Use logical reasoning

Materials

- *Figure It* (page 47; figureit.pdf)
- Counters (*optional*)
- *Student Response Form* (page 130; studentresponse.pdf) (*optional*)

Activate

1. Show students the equation $\bigcirc + \bigcirc = 8$ and tell them that each circle stands for the same number.

2. Ask *How could we figure out the value of the circle?* Several students may recognize that $4 + 4 = 8$ and say they just know the answer. Probe deeper by asking *What could you do if you didn't know it?* or *What could you suggest to a friend who did not recognize this fact?* or *How could we use counters to help us?*

3. Challenge students' thinking by asking if the circle can stand for any other number. (*No, because it must represent one number, and four is the only number that makes eight when added to itself.*)

Solve

1. Distribute copies of *Figure It* to students. Have students work in pairs or in small groups so that they can talk about their thinking. Explain that their job is to find the values of the shapes. Remind them that the same shape stands for the same number.

2. As the students work, ask clarifying or refocusing questions, for example *What does it mean when the same symbol is shown again?*

Debrief

1. Who can show us how they found their answer?

2. How might thinking about doubles help you solve these problems?

3. Direct students' attention to the second line of the above-level problem. What do you notice about this equation? What does the equal sign tell us?

Differentiate ▢

Some students may be able to solve the above-level problem if the second statement is written as $\star + 5 = \bigoplus$. Rewrite the clue for these students and have them solve the problem. Over time, include other examples of equations written in the original format.

Figure It

Each shape stands for one number.

☺ + ☺ = 6

☺ + 2 = _____

Figure It

Each shape stands for one number.

◇ + ◇ = 6

10 = ★ + ★

◇ + ★ = _____

Figure It

Each shape stands for one number.

⋈ + ⋈ + ⋈ = 9

⊕ + ⋈ + ⋈ = 6

⋈ + ⊕ = _____

At the Party Store

Standards

- Solves real-world problems involving addition and subtraction of whole numbers
- Understands the inverse relationship between addition and subtraction

Overview

Students use the taking-apart model of subtraction to solve story problems.

Problem-Solving Strategies

- Act it out or use manipulatives
- Count, compute, or write an equation
- Guess and check or make an estimate

Materials

- *At the Party Store* (page 49; partystore.pdf)
- counters
- *Student Response Form* (page 130; studentresponse.pdf) *(optional)*

Activate

1. On the board, sketch a picture of five striped party hats and three polka dot hats. Ask students what they see, and what equation they can write about what they see. Ask *Is there another equation you could write?* Students are most likely to suggest an addition sentence. If no one shares a subtraction sentence, ask *Can anyone see 8 – 5 = 3? Is there another subtraction sentence you can see?*

Solve

1. Distribute copies of *At the Party Store* to students and make counters available. Have students work alone or in pairs.

2. Before debriefing you may wish students to place their work on their desks and take a walk to see how others recorded their thinking. As students take this gallery walk, listen to their comments to learn what they notice and what connections they make.

Debrief

1. How did you find the answer to the problem?

2. Did anyone find it a different way?

3. What equation did you write? What other equation would also make sense?

Differentiate ⬤ ▢ △ ☆

Some students will be able to find the answer to a problem, but will not be able to write an equation to represent it. Questions such as *What do you know? What do you need to find out?* can help students make connections between a story problem and its corresponding equation.

At the Party Store

Michael buys 7 balloons.

Five of the balloons are small.

The rest are large.

How many of the balloons are large?

Write an equation for this problem.

At the Party Store

Jillian buys 13 candles.

Some of the candles are red.

The other 6 candles are blue.

How many candles are red?

Write an equation for this problem.

At the Party Store

Ms. Watson buys some T-shirts to paint.

She gives 9 of the T-shirts to her children to paint.

She has 7 of the T-shirts left.

How many T-shirts did Ms. Watson buy?

Write an equation for this problem.

Get a Prize

Standards

- Adds and subtracts whole numbers
- Solves real-world problems involving addition and subtraction of whole numbers

Overview

In this problem set students identify the prizes that they can get for a given number of carnival tickets.

Problem-Solving Strategies

- Count, compute, or write an equation
- Find information in a picture, list, table, graph, or diagram
- Guess and check or make an estimate

Materials

- *Get a Prize* (page 51; getprize.pdf)
- counters
- *Student Response Form* (page 130; studentresponse.pdf) *(optional)*

Activate

1. Ask students if they have ever won a prize. Allow two or three students to share their stories. If no one mentions getting a prize with carnival tickets, do so yourself.

2. On the board, sketch several items that students could win at a carnival, and label them with different ticket costs. For example, a ball labeled *4 tickets*, a bracelet labeled *5 tickets*, and an eraser labeled *3 tickets*. Ask students to identify the number of tickets it takes to get each of the items. Ask *How many tickets do you need to get two erasers? What could you get with 9 tickets?*

Solve

1. Distribute copies of *Get a Prize* to students. Have students work alone or in pairs. Tell them that the pictures show new prizes that you can get with carnival tickets. Make sure students understand that below each picture is the number of tickets needed to buy the prize. Have counters available for students to use.

2. Observe students as they work. Do they use their fingers to find the totals, appear to use mental arithmetic, or record numbers and check their sums?

3. Provide descriptive feedback to students such as *I see you checking your ideas.*

Debrief

1. How did you find the prizes that matched the number of tickets you used?

2. When we guess and check to find an answer, how can we make smart guesses?

3. How could solving the on-level problem help us to solve the above-level one?

Differentiate ◯ ☆

Students who have difficulty writing can work with a partner who can record the answers on one sheet. You may also want to make an extra copy of the activity sheet and have students cut out the pictures. Students can then move the items closer together when checking guesses.

Get a Prize

Collect carnival tickets to win a prize.

The signs tell you the number of tickets you need for each prize.

yo-yo

jump rope

pencil

car

You use 6 tickets.

You get a _____ and a _____.

Get a Prize

Collect carnival tickets to win a prize.

The signs tell you the number of tickets you need for each prize.

yo-yo

jump rope

pencil

car

You use 10 tickets.

You get a _____ and a _____.

Get a Prize

Collect carnival tickets to win a prize.

The signs tell you the number of tickets you need for each prize.

yo-yo

jump rope

pencil

car

You use 15 tickets.

You get a _____ and a _____ and a _____.

On the Line

Standards
- Counts whole numbers
- Understands symbolic, concrete, and pictorial representations of numbers

Overview
This problem set focuses on modeling addition, or counting up, on number lines. Students model the hops of an animal on the line and identify the number where the animal lands or how many hops it takes for the animal to get to a given point on the line.

Problem-Solving Strategies
- Count, compute, or write an equation
- Find information in a picture, list, table, graph, or diagram
- Organize information in a picture, list, table, graph, or diagram

Materials
- *On the Line* (page 53; online.pdf)
- *Number Line 0–20* (numberline20.pdf)
- large number line to place on the classroom floor (*optional*)
- *Student Response Form* (page 130; studentresponse.pdf) (*optional*)

Activate
1. Ask students to identify animals that hop. If no one identifies a frog, bunny, or kangaroo, do so yourself. Have students name the animal they think takes the longest hop.

2. If you have a floor-size number line, have a student imitate one of the animals jumping on the number line by ones, and then by twos, while the class calls out the numbers.

3. Distribute copies of *Number Line 0–20* to students. Have students place their fingers on the mark for *0* and make a hop that is three spaces long. Ask students where they landed. (*3*) Repeat several times using different hop lengths or different start numbers.

Solve
1. Distribute copies of *On the Line* to students and review the directions. Have students work in pairs and encourage them to talk about their thinking.

2. Encourage students as they work with descriptive feedback, such as *I see you are making each hop carefully. I notice you are double-checking your hops on the number line.*

Debrief
1. How does working together help you to solve problems?

2. How did you keep track of the animal's jumps?

3. Why is a number line a good tool to use while you solve these problems?

Differentiate ○ □ △ ☆
Some students may need to make a mark after each hop to help them keep track of their movement on the number line. Other students may have more success working with a large number line on which they can walk.

On the Line

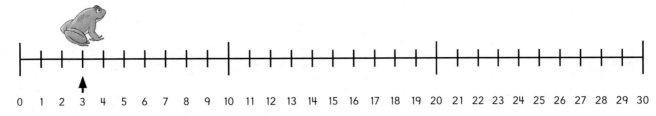

0 1 2 3 4 5 6 7 8 9 10 11 12 13 14 15 16 17 18 19 20 21 22 23 24 25 26 27 28 29 30

Tam is at 3.

Tam makes hops that are 1 space long.

She makes 4 hops.

On what number does Tam land?

On the Line

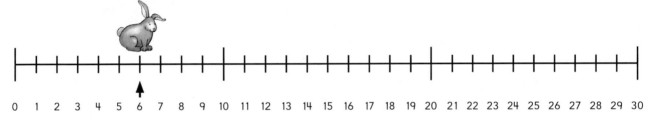

0 1 2 3 4 5 6 7 8 9 10 11 12 13 14 15 16 17 18 19 20 21 22 23 24 25 26 27 28 29 30

Ben makes hops that are 2 spaces long.

He makes 3 hops.

On what number does Ben land?

On the Line

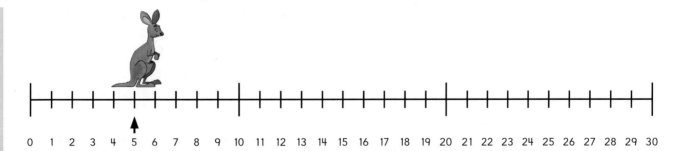

0 1 2 3 4 5 6 7 8 9 10 11 12 13 14 15 16 17 18 19 20 21 22 23 24 25 26 27 28 29 30

Kim makes hops that are 4 spaces long.

She wants to get to 17.

How many hops does Kim need to make?

Which Numbers?

Standards

- Adds and subtracts whole numbers
- Understands the inverse relationship between addition and subtraction

Overview

In this problem set students choose numbers to make equations true.

Problem-Solving Strategies

- Act it out or use manipulatives
- Count, compute, or write an equation
- Guess and check or make an estimate

Materials

- *Which Numbers?* (page 55; whichnumbers.pdf)
- counters
- sticky notes *(optional)*
- *Student Response Form* (page 130; studentresponse.pdf) *(optional)*

Activate

1. Display the following on the board:

   _____ + _____ = 5

3	1	2

2. Ask *Which numbers from the box could we use to make the equation true?* Once students agree on an answer, ask *How could we check to make sure we are right? What would be an equation that is not true?*

Solve

1. Distribute copies of *Which Numbers?* to students. Have students work alone or in pairs. Have counters available for students who wish to use them.

2. Point out the numbers in the boxes. Make sure students understand that they must use these numbers in their equations.

Debrief

1. What equation did you write?

2. How did you find the numbers that made the equation true?

3. How might making a guess help someone find the answer?

4. Did anyone find another order for the numbers? Will this always work?

Differentiate

Students' solution methods will vary. A few students may immediately recognize the correct numbers for a given sum or difference, while others will guess and check different combinations until they find one that is correct. Some students will use the counters to guess and check, some will write different number combinations and then add or subtract to check, while others will guess and check mentally. Sticky notes with these numbers on them may make it easier for students to arrange the numbers to guess and check their equations.

Which Numbers? ○

Use two of the numbers below. Make the equation true.

| 6 | 8 | 3 |

_____ + _____ = 9

Which Numbers? ☐

Use two of the numbers below. Make the equation true.

| 12 | 7 | 8 | 10 |

_____ − _____ = 2

Find another way.

_____ − _____ = 2

Which Numbers? ◁

Use each of the numbers below. Make the equations true.

| 5 | 12 | 8 | 4 |

13 = _____ + _____

_____ − 8 = _____

Toss It

Standard

Adds and subtracts whole numbers

Overview

Students combine possible scores on a bean bag toss board to get a given total number of points. The students are expected to find multiple solutions for each problem.

Problem-Solving Strategies

- Count, compute, or write an equation
- Guess and check or make an estimate
- Organize information in a picture, list, table, graph, or diagram

Materials

- *Toss It* (page 57; tossit.pdf)
- one number sign for each of the numbers: 1, 2, 3, 4, and 5
- small number cards for the numbers: 1, 2, 3, 4, 5, 6,7, 8 (*optional*)
- *Student Response Form* (page 130; studentresponse.pdf) (*optional*)

Activate

1. Ask students what they would tell someone who wants to know what the word *total* means.

2. Have five students wear one of the number signs and stand facing the other students. Say *We want to see numbers with a total of five. Which two children should step forward?* Have the two named children step forward and have the other students add to check. Ask *Is there another way?* If someone suggests having just the five come forward, remind students that two numbers are needed.

Solve

1. Distribute copies of *Toss It* to students. Have students work alone, in pairs, or in small groups.

2. As students work, ask clarifying and refocusing questions such as *Can you show me which numbers you tried? What did you mean when you said that some of the numbers on the board cannot be used?*

Debrief

1. What ways did you find?

2. What did you do to find another way after you found one answer?

3. How did you keep track of numbers you had tried already?

Differentiate ◯ ■ △ ☆

Some students might find it easier to guess and check combinations of numbers if the numbers could be moved together. Give these students number cards to use. Students ready for a greater challenge should be encouraged to systemize their guessing and checking. Encourage them to think about whether their guess was too high or too low.

Toss It ○

You toss two bags.

What two scores give you 6 total points?

List two ways.

_____ and _____

_____ and _____

Toss It ▢

You toss two bags.
Each bag gets a different score.
The total number of points you get is greater than 8.
What two scores did the bags get?
List three ways.

_____ and _____

_____ and _____

_____ and _____

Toss It △

You toss two bags.

Each bag gets a different score.

Which two scores give you 10 or more total points?

List all the ways.

Where Did You Start?

Standards

- Adds and subtracts whole numbers
- Understands the inverse relationship between addition and subtraction

Overview

Students are presented with a series of computational steps and the result. The students' task is to use addition and subtraction to find the starting number.

Problem-Solving Strategies

- Count, compute, or write an equation
- Guess and check or make an estimate
- Work backward

Materials

- *Where Did You Start?* (page 59; wherestart.pdf)
- *Number Board* (numberboard.pdf)
- *Student Response Form* (page 130; studentresponse.pdf) *(optional)*

Activate

1. Distribute copies of *Number Board* and display it for students. Tell students that they are going on number "trips." Say *You start at 6. You add 3. Where does your trip end?* Model the trip first and then have students model it on their activity sheets. When students are ready, include two addition moves or one or two subtraction moves.

2. Describe the trips without the start number. For example *You start on a number. You add 5. Your trip ends at 10. Where did you start?* Repeat with two addition moves and then consider trips involving subtraction.

Solve

1. Distribute copies of *Where Did You Start?* to students. Have students work alone, in pairs, or in small groups.

2. As students work ask refocusing questions such as *How could thinking about addition or subtraction help you find the start numbers?*

Debrief

1. How could subtraction help you to find the answer to the problem?

2. How might combining steps help you?

3. What equation could we write to represent this part or all of the trip?

Differentiate ⬤

Inverse reasoning can be particularly challenging for some students. Encourage them to make a guess and then act out the problem to check. Over time, extra work with fact families may help students make these links. Writing an equation such as □ + 4 = 6 can also be helpful to students.

Where Did You Start? ◯

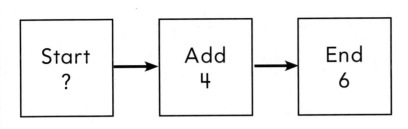

? = _____

Where Did You Start? ▢

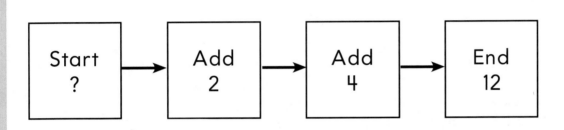

? = _____

Where Did You Start? △

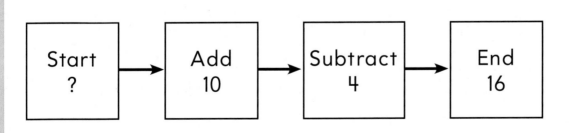

? = _____

Ask a Question

Standard
Adds and subtracts whole numbers

Overview
Posing questions is the focus of this problem set. The data given suggest questions related to joining, separating, and comparing groups.

Problem-Solving Strategies
- Count, compute, or write an equation
- Guess and check or make an estimate

Materials
- *Ask a Question* (page 61; askquestion.pdf)
- 6 pencils
- 2 erasers
- *Student Response Form* (page 130; studentresponse.pdf) *(optional)*

Activate

1. Have a volunteer dramatize whispering something in your ear. Then say *My answer to this question is Monday. What do you think (volunteer's name) asked me?* Encourage students to brainstorm a variety of questions.

2. Repeat step 1, but replace the answer *Monday* with the answer 5. Again, have students brainstorm a number of ideas such as *What is the number of toes on a foot? What is the number after four? How many people live with me? What is 2 + 3?*

3. Show students a collection of 6 pencils and 2 erasers. Have another student pretend to whisper in your ear, then say *My answer is 2. What question about the pencils and erasers do you think (student's name) asked me?* Repeat the process for the answer 6.

4. Challenge students with the answer *4*. (*How many more pencils are there than erasers? How many fewer erasers are there than pencils?*) As the questions for this answer are not as obvious, some students may pose questions unrelated to the sets. Explain that the question must be about these pencils and erasers.

Solve

1. Distribute copies of *Ask a Question* to students and have students work in pairs to encourage discussions.

2. Observe the partners as they work. Do they both contribute equally and listen well?

Debrief

1. What question did you find?

2. Did anyone ask a different question for that answer?

3. What helped you to think of questions?

Differentiate

Some students will find it easier to identify questions when they model the data with pictures, real items, or colored counters.

Ask a Question

Use the information to write a question for each answer.

Ned has 3 pencils.

Sarah has 2 pencils.

Answers:	5	1

Ask a Question

Use the information to write a question for each answer.

Belle has 3 crayons and 2 markers.

Mark has 4 crayons.

Answers:	5	9	1

Ask a Question

Use the information to write a question for each answer.

Lexi has 2 erasers and 4 pencils.

Renaldo has 3 erasers and 4 pencils.

Answers:	1	5	8	0

How Many Animals?

Standard

Solves real-world problems involving addition and subtraction of whole numbers

Overview

This problem set focuses on finding ways to compose a number. The total number of animals and the two types of animals are given. The students are to determine the possible number of each type of animal. Students find one or multiple solutions.

Problem-Solving Strategies

- Count, compute, or write an equation
- Guess and check or make an estimate

Materials

- *How Many Animals?* (page 63; animals.pdf)
- color tiles, connecting cubes, or counters of different colors
- *Student Response Form* (page 130; studentresponse.pdf) *(optional)*

Activate

1. Set out the manipulatives for pairs of students. Tell each partner to pick a different color, such as yellow or red. Each partner takes a handful of counters of his or her color. Say *Make a group of five from your counters. There must be at least one counter from each of you.* Have a student restate the directions and give the students time to make their group. Ask *How many reds and yellows are in your group? How could we write that in an equation? Did anyone find a different way? How could we show this other way in an equation?*

2. Repeat step 1 for a group of six counters.

Solve

1. Distribute copies of *How Many Animals?* to students. Have students work alone, in pairs, or in small groups.

2. Encourage students to find other solutions. Ask *Is there another way you can find that amount?*

Debrief

1. What answers did you find?

2. How might one answer help us find another one?

3. Do we have all of the possibilities? How do we know?

Differentiate ○ □ △ ☆

These open-ended problems allow for a variety of responses. Some students will find one set of addends and some will find several. Other students will find all of the solutions through a somewhat random approach, while some will work in an organized manner. Students who work systematically with small numbers may not do so with larger numbers. It is worth returning to this type of problem over time to document student growth. If you change the total number in each problem, the level of challenge will be significantly different.

How Many Animals?

There are 8 pets in the store.

Some of the pets are cats.

The other pets are dogs.

How many cats are there?

How many dogs are there?

How Many Animals?

There are 10 fish in the tank.

Some of the fish are guppies.

The other fish are goldfish.

How many guppies are there?

How many goldfish are there?

How Many Animals?

There are 12 animals in the picture.

Some of the animals are lions.

The other animals are tigers.

How many lions are there?

How many tigers are there?

How Many Pennies?

Standard

Solves real-world problems involving addition and subtraction of whole numbers

Overview

These problems require students to work backward to find the number of pennies someone has.

Problem-Solving Strategies

- Act it out or use manipulatives
- Count, compute, or write an equation
- Work backward

Materials

- *How Many Pennies?* (page 65; pennies.pdf)
- pennies (real or play money)
- *Student Response Form* (page 130; studentresponse.pdf) (*optional*)

Activate

1. Call on two students to model a problem with you. Give the first student ten pennies privately so that the other students cannot see how many you gave. Say *(First student's name) has four more pennies than (second student's name).* Give the second student six pennies, counting aloud as you do so and recording the number for students to see. Have a student restate the information and then ask students to talk in pairs to identify how many pennies the first student has. Ask *How many pennies does (first student's name) have? How did you decide? How can you check your answer?*

2. To show students how to check their thinking, retell the same story, but have the first student show and tell the number of pennies.

3. Repeat and include an example with the first student having fewer pennies than the second one.

Solve

1. Distribute copies of *How Many Pennies?* to students. Have students work in pairs or in small groups so that they can dramatize the problem(s) from the beginning to check their thinking. Distribute pennies so students can model the situations.

2. As students work ask clarifying questions, such as *What information do you have? What question are you trying to answer? How can you model this situation?*

Debrief

1. How did you find your answer?

2. Why might someone call these working backward problems?

3. How might you convince someone your answer is correct?

Differentiate ◯ ▢ ☆

In these problems, the information students need to use first is given last. To help students who are confused by this order, you may want to draw an arrow that starts beside the last piece of data and points up.

How Many Pennies?

Emma has 3 more pennies than Sasha.

Sasha has   .

How many pennies does Emma have?

How Many Pennies?

Logan has 8 more pennies than Aiden.

Aiden has 3 more pennies than Ella.

Ella has   .

How many pennies does Aiden have?

How many pennies does Logan have?

How Many Pennies?

Miguel has 9 more pennies than Lei.

Lei has 4 fewer pennies than Massie.

Massie has 12 pennies.

How many pennies does Miguel have?

Hands, Toes, and Legs

Standards

- Adds and subtracts whole numbers
- Recognizes regularities in a variety of contexts
- Extends simple patterns

Overview

In this problem set students complete tables to determine the number of hands, toes, or legs associated with a given number of people or dogs.

Problem-Solving Strategies

- Act it out or use manipulatives
- Count, compute, or write an equation
- Find information in a picture, list, table, graph, or diagram

Materials

- *Hands, Toes, and Legs* (page 67; handstoeslegs.pdf)
- counters
- *Student Response Form* (page 130; studentresponse.pdf) *(optional)*

Activate

1. Pose the question *What are some ways you can count to ten?* If no one suggests it, model counting by twos.

2. Invite one student to stand in front of the others. Ask *How many people do you see? How many eyes do you see?* Invite a second student to join the first student and repeat the two questions. Model counting the eyes by ones to check. Ask if there is another way we could count the eyes.

3. Invite a third student to join the other two and repeat the two questions. This time have students demonstrate two different ways to count to check. Then summarize the data in a table.

4. Have students predict the number of eyes there will be when there are four students standing. Check the prediction by inviting a fourth student to join the group and again have students count by ones and twos.

Solve

1. Distribute copies of *Hands, Toes, and Legs* to students. Have students work alone, in pairs, or in small groups.

Debrief

1. What did you do to complete the table?

2. Did anyone do it a different way?

3. How do tables help us find answers to questions like these?

Differentiate △

Though many students can count by twos and tens, it is unlikely that first graders count by fours. Students can complete the above-level table by using counters, drawings, or by counting on to the previous answer. All methods are acceptable and support a discussion about different ways to solve problems.

Hands, Toes, and Legs

People	Hands
1	2
2	4
3	6
4	

Hannah made a table to show the number of people and hands.

Complete the table. How many hands do 4 people have?

Hands, Toes, and Legs

People	Toes
1	10
2	
3	
4	
5	

Jayden made a table to show the number of people and toes.

Complete the table. How many toes do 5 people have?

Hands, Toes, and Legs

Dogs	Legs
1	
2	
3	
4	
5	
6	

Olivia made a table to show the number of dogs and legs.

Complete the table. How many legs do 6 dogs have?

Show It

Standards

- Makes organized lists or tables of information necessary for solving a problem
- Understands symbolic, concrete, and pictorial representations of numbers

Overview

This problem set focuses on representing numbers using tens and ones.

Problem-Solving Strategies

- Act it out or use manipulatives
- Count, compute, or write an equation
- Organize information in a picture, list, table, graph, or diagram

Materials

- *Show It* (page 69; showit.pdf)
- base-ten blocks (tens and ones)
- *Student Response Form* (page 130; studentresponse.pdf) *(optional)*

Activate

1. Write the number *17* on the board. Ask students how they could show this number with base-ten blocks.

2. Place three tens in one open hand and three ones in another open hand. Ask a volunteer to take a few pieces from each hand. Have the student show the others these pieces and write the number represented on the board. For example, if the student took two tens and three ones, he or she would write 23.

3. Replace the used pieces in your hands and repeat step 2 with other volunteers, asking them to take a different set of pieces each time.

Solve

1. Distribute copies of *Show It* to students. Have students work alone, in pairs, or in small groups. Make sure all students understand the directions and have access to base-ten blocks for tens and ones.

2. Ask questions as students work, such as *Why did you choose this number? What would happen if you used this number? Will any number work?*

Debrief

1. How did you find your answers? Did anyone do it differently?

2. What numbers could you show if you only had 3 tens pieces?

3. How did you know you found all the numbers? Is there another way to organize the numbers you found?

Differentiate ⚪ ⬜

To help students become more independent problem solvers, let them find their own ways to organize data. At this grade level, it is all right if they do not identify all of the possibilities. If some students require more structure for success, you might start a table for them (with headings of tens and ones), which they can complete.

Show It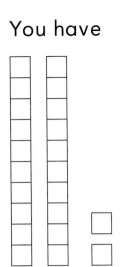

You have

Use tens and ones. Use at least one of each kind of block.

What numbers can you show?

Write them.

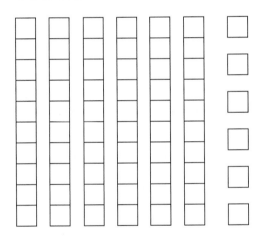

Show It

You have

Use the tens and all of the ones.

What numbers can you show?

Write them.

Show It

You have

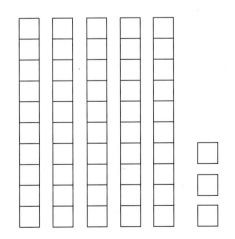

Use tens and ones.

Use more tens than ones.

What numbers can you show?

Write them.

Sticker Stories

Standards

- Adds and subtracts whole numbers
- Solves real-world problems involving addition and subtraction of whole numbers
- Understands the inverse relationship between addition and subtraction

Overview

In this problem set students participate in the process of posing problems. They are given word problems without numbers and write numbers that fit the story.

Problem-Solving Strategies

- Count, compute, or write an equation
- Guess and check or make an estimate
- Simplify the problem

Materials

- *Sticker Stories* (page 71; stickerstories.pdf)
- *Student Response Form* (page 130; studentresponse.pdf) *(optional)*

Activate

1. To assess students' number relationships, display the problem below. Read the story a couple of times to students as they follow along.

   Matt has 25 stickers.

   He gets 1 more sticker.

   Now he has 26 stickers.

2. Erase 25 and 1, and ask students to suggest other numbers that would work in this story.

3. Repeat step 2, replacing the numbers with a different set of two numbers.

Solve

1. Distribute copies of *Sticker Stories* to students. Tell them these are other sticker stories for them to complete. Have students work in pairs or small groups to encourage them to discuss different ways to complete the stories.

2. Ask refocusing and clarifying questions as the students work, such as *Will the person in the story have more or less stickers when the story starts? What do you know about the number of stickers in this problem?*

Debrief

1. Who found an answer for this story? Did someone find a different answer?

2. Why do you think there are so many correct answers?

3. What are some ways to find numbers that make sense in these stories?

Differentiate ⬤ ◼ △ ☆

You may wish to encourage some students to simplify the problem by replacing the given number with a smaller one. The change may help these students recognize the relationship among the numbers. Other students may enjoy the challenge of finding several solutions.

Sticker Stories

Fill in the blanks with numbers to make the story true.

Jan has _____ stickers.

She gets _____ more stickers.

Now she has 30 stickers.

Sticker Stories

Fill in the blanks with numbers to make the story true.

Liam has _____ stickers.

He gives his sister 20 stickers.

Now he has _____ stickers.

Sticker Stories

Fill in the blanks with numbers to make the story true.

Nick has _____ stickers.

He gets _____ more stickers.

Then he gives his friend 40 stickers.

Now he has _____ stickers.

Tile Patterns

Standards

- Counts whole numbers
- Understands symbolic, concrete, and pictorial representations of numbers
- Extends simple patterns

Overview

Students are given number patterns to extend and then decide which of the new numbers will be shaded.

Problem-Solving Strategies

- Count, compute, or write an equation
- Find information in a picture, list, table, graph, or diagram

Materials

- *Tile Patterns* (page 73; tilepatterns.pdf)
- color tiles
- *Number Line 0–120* (numberline120.pdf) *(optional)*
- *Student Response Form* (page 130; studentresponse.pdf) *(optional)*

Activate

1. Have students describe a tile pattern they have seen. Ask them where they saw it and what they can tell us about the pattern.

2. Have students practice counting backward as a group, first starting at 19, then starting at 45, and then 104.

Solve

1. Distribute copies of *Tile Patterns* to students and make sure students understand the directions. Have students work alone, in pairs, or in small groups. Have color tiles available for those who wish to build the patterns.

2. While students are working, observe and make note of those who are struggling, those who are using "accountable talk," and those who are relying heavily on the thinking of others.

Debrief

1. What missing numbers did you write?

2. How did you decide which numbers to shade?

3. How could you predict the next shaded number?

Differentiate ◯ ▢ △ ☆

Some students will be better able to identify and extend the numerical sequence. Others will be better able to find and extend the visual pattern of the shaded numbers. Working together can help both types of learners experience success. Most students find it more challenging to count backward than forward. You may wish to make *Number Line 0–120* available as a reference. Assemble the number line for students in advance.

Tile Patterns

Write the missing numbers in the tiles. Shade the tiles to show the pattern.

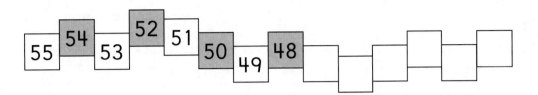

Tile Patterns

Write the missing numbers in the tiles. Shade the tiles to show the pattern.

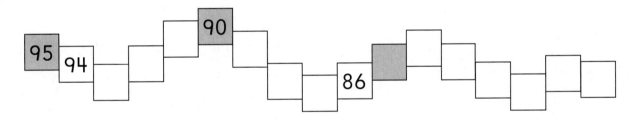

Tile Patterns

Write the missing numbers in the tiles. Shade the tiles to show the pattern.

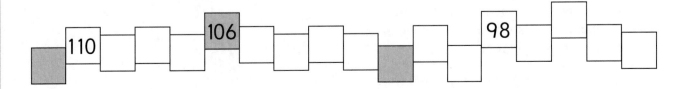

More or Less

Standard

Uses base-ten concepts to compare and represent whole numbers in flexible ways

Overview

In these problems, two children are introduced who each have a set of tens, ones, or tens and ones. Students decide which set represents a greater number. They then record the two numbers and the relationship between them using the greater than and less than signs.

Problem-Solving Strategies

- Act it out or use manipulatives
- Count, compute, or write an equation
- Use logical reasoning

Materials

- *More or Less* (page 75; moreless.pdf)
- base-ten blocks
- *Place Value Mat* (placevalue.pdf) (*optional*)
- *Student Response Form* (page 130; studentresponse.pdf) (*optional*)

Activate

1. Using base-ten blocks, show students one set of 11 ones and another set of one ten. Ask students which set shows the greater number, and how they know. Ask them how we can use the greater than and less than signs to show this relationship.

2. Repeat step 1 using a set of two tens and nine ones and a set of three tens, and asking about the number that is less.

3. Distribute the base-ten blocks to students and have them work in pairs. Direct each student to take a random set of tens and ones. Then have them compare their sets to decide which is greater and which is less.

Solve

1. Distribute copies of *More or Less* to students. Have students work alone, in pairs, or in small groups.

2. Observe whether students trade tens for ones, or record the standard numerals.

Debrief

1. Who can tell us how they found an answer?

2. How might the base-ten blocks be helpful?

3. How does thinking about trading (or bundling) help you?

4. How do you remember which sign stands for less than and which stands for greater than?

Differentiate

Some students may need a graphic organizer to help them record appropriately. Distribute *Place Value Mat* to help these students organize the tens and ones when they model the sets.

More or Less ◯

Nima has 36 ones.

Roberto has 4 tens and 2 ones.

Whose blocks show the greater number?

Write the numbers and > to show which is greater.

More or Less ◻

Misha has 5 tens and 12 ones.

Sophia has 6 tens.

Whose blocks show the number that is less?

Write the numbers and < to show which is less.

More or Less ◁

Carmen has 6 tens and 24 ones.

Salim has 8 tens and 3 ones.

Whose blocks show the greater number?

Write the numbers and > to show which is greater.

Now use the numbers and < to show which is less.

Shrinking Machines

Standards
- Adds and subtracts whole numbers
- Extends simple patterns

Overview
Students are shown input and output values. They find the relationship between these values and use that pattern to find the missing value.

Problem-Solving Strategies
- Count, compute, or write an equation
- Find information in a picture, list, table, graph, or diagram
- Generalize a pattern

Materials
- *Shrinking Machines* (page 77; shrinking.pdf)
- base-ten blocks
- *Student Response Form* (page 130; studentresponse.pdf) *(optional)*

Activate

1. Display a T-chart with columns labeled *In* and *Out* for students. Explain that numbers will go in and come out differently. You may wish to discuss the idea of a function machine, in which a number goes in, an operation happens, and a different number comes out.

2. Ask a student to name a number greater than ten. Record the number in the *In* column and write the number one less in the *Out* column. Repeat with other numbers the students name.

3. When students think they know how the numbers are being changed, write a number that goes in and have the students identify what comes out.

4. Have students describe how the numbers are changing. Encourage descriptions in words (e.g., *they are one less; subtract one*) and with symbols (e.g., – 1).

Solve

1. Distribute copies of *Shrinking Machines* to students. Have students work alone or in pairs. Ask clarifying and refocusing questions to make sure students understand that they are to find the missing number and to describe how the numbers are being changed.

2. Ask refocusing questions such as *What do you notice about how this number changes?*

Debrief

1. What did you find for the missing number?

2. What is this machine doing to all of the numbers? How can you explain what is happening in words? How can you show it using symbols?

Differentiate

Encourage students to use base-ten blocks to model an input number and then decide what to do to show the associated output number. Have them do this for each pair of numbers in a table until they can predict the final number's output.

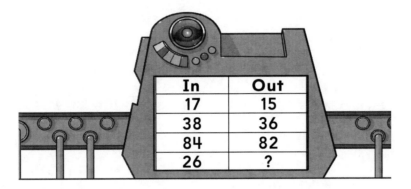

Shrinking Machines

In	Out
30	20
50	40
20	10
40	?

? = _____

What does this machine do?

Shrinking Machines

In	Out
17	15
38	36
84	82
26	?

? = _____

What does this machine do?

Shrinking Machines

In	Out
26	21
17	12
58	53
?	75

? = _____

What does this machine do?

Number Stories

Standard

Understands that numerals are symbols used to represent quantities or attributes of real-world objects

Overview

In this problem set, students choose from a set of numbers to complete stories in a way that makes sense.

Problem-Solving Strategies

- Count, compute, or write an equation
- Guess and check or make an estimate
- Use logical reasoning

Materials

- *Number Stories* (page 79; numberstories.pdf)
- *Student Response Form* (page 130; studentresponse.pdf) *(optional)*

Activate

1. To assess students' number sense of data in real-world situations, display the following story:

   I am 8 years old. My younger sister is 10 years old. I am 4 years old and in the tenth grade.

2. Ask students if these sentences make sense. Have students suggest what to change so that they do make sense. Encourage students to find more than one solution.

Solve

1. Distribute copies of *Number Stories* to students. Read the problems with students first and then have them work alone, in pairs, or in small groups.

2. As students work, ask clarifying and refocusing questions such as *How do you know this story makes sense? Are there more children or chairs in our classroom?*

Debrief

1. What number did you find easiest to place? Why?

2. What suggestions could you give to a friend who needed help placing the numbers in problems like these?

3. Think about the number of students, teachers, and crayons in a classroom. Which number would be least? Greatest?

Differentiate ◯ ▢ △ ☆

Students who have a good sense of number relationships may not be the same students who are successful readers. Pairing students with different strengths can be beneficial to both types of students.

Number Stories

Use each number from the box below once to complete the story.

8	6	93

All About Kim

Kim is _____ years old. Kim's older brother is _____ years old. Kim lives at _____ Pine Street.

Use each number from the box below once to complete the story.

6	2	8	3

All About Jed

Jed has _____ brothers. Jed has _____ sisters. Jed has more brothers than sisters. There are _____ children in Jed's family. There are _____ people in Jed's family.

Use each number from the box below once to complete the story.

26	7	4	29	1

All About Lin

Lin is _____ years old. Lin is in grade _____. There are _____ chairs in her classroom. There are _____ tables in her classroom. There are _____ students in Lin's classroom.

T-Shirt Numbers

Standard

Uses base-ten concepts to compare and represent whole numbers in flexible ways

Overview

In this problem set, students use clues to find the number on each child's T-shirt. The numbers are represented in a variety of formats.

Problem-Solving Strategies

- Count, compute, or write an equation
- Use logical reasoning

Materials

- *T-Shirt Numbers* (page 81; tshirt.pdf)
- *Student Response Form* (page 130; studentresponse.pdf) *(optional)*

Activate

1. Display the number *24*. Invite a volunteer to show the number using tens and ones. Ask one or two other students to show the number a different way. If not suggested by students, include a drawing of base-ten blocks to show *24*, and expanded notation *(20 + 4)*.

2. Repeat step 1 for the number *17* and then for 56.

3. Ask *Do any of you have T-shirts with numbers written on them? Why do you think members of sport teams wear numbers on their shirts?*

Solve

1. Distribute copies of *T-shirt Numbers* to students. Have students work alone, in pairs, or in small groups. Tell them that their job is to find the name of the child wearing each shirt. Make sure students understand that the clues will help them decide who is wearing which number.

2. As students are working, ask questions such as *What do you notice about the tens? How confident are you in your answers? Why?*

3. Encourage students with descriptive feedback such as *I hear you trying to help your partner.*

Debrief

1. Who can tell us how they found an answer?

2. Did someone use the clues in a different order?

3. Did you always have to look at the tens and ones to find the number that matched a clue?

4. Did it matter which way a number was shown?

Differentiate ⬤ △

Some students may find it easier to write each of the numbers in standard form before they read the clues. Students ready for a greater challenge may enjoy creating their own clues for the numbers 25, 32, and 39.

T-Shirt Numbers

$20 + 8$ 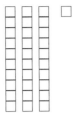   23

Jen has the greatest number.

Loni has the least number.

Mark has number 28.

Write the names.

_____ _____ _____

T-Shirt Numbers

   43 $30 + 8$

Manny's number is equal to $20 + 3$.

Sam does not have the least number.

Ava's number has 3 tens.

Write the names.

_____ _____ _____

T-Shirt Numbers

$40 + 4$ 43 $30 + 3$ 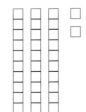

Mini has a number with 4 tens.

Ann has the greatest number.

Joe's number is less than Bailey's number.

Write the names.

_____ _____ _____ _____

June Birthdays

Standards

- Understands symbolic, concrete, and pictorial representations of numbers
- Uses base-ten concepts to compare and represent whole numbers in flexible ways

Overview

In this problem set, students are shown a calendar and use clues to identify birthday dates. The clues involve the names of the days and the order of the numbers.

Problem-Solving Strategies

- Find information in a picture, list, table, graph, or diagram
- Use logical reasoning

Materials

- *June Birthdays* (page 83; junebdays.pdf)
- classroom calendar
- *Student Response Form* (page 130; studentresponse.pdf) *(optional)*

Activate

1. Have students focus on the classroom calendar and read aloud the days of the week as a group. Then, ask *What day of the week is it today? What day of the week is tomorrow? Where does the calendar tell us the names of the days? What dates are on Mondays this month? What is today's date? What will be the date tomorrow?*

2. Ask if anyone has a birthday this month. If so, have the student point to the date on the calendar. If no student has a birthday this month, tell students that you have a friend with a birthday on (name the date) and point to the date. Ask *Is (child's or friend's name) birthday before (month) 20? After (month) 15?*

Solve

1. Distribute copies of *June Birthdays* to students and have students with June birthdays identity themselves. Tell students that they are going to learn about other June birthdays. Have students work alone, in pairs, or in small groups.

2. As students work, ask questions such as *What does this clue tell you?*

Debrief

1. What birthday date did you find?

2. How did the clues help you identify the birthday?

3. Flag Day is June 14. What clues could we write for someone to use to find this date?

Differentiate

Some students are challenged by keeping track of the dates eliminated by a clue. Encourage these students to cross off the dates on the calendar when they are no longer possible. Some students may find it easier to work with the larger numerals on the classroom calendar.

June Birthdays

June						
Sun.	Mon.	Tues.	Wed.	Thurs.	Fri.	Sat.
		1	2	3	4	5
6	7	8	9	10	11	12
13	14	15	16	17	18	19
20	21	22	23	24	25	26
27	28	29	30			

Brianna's birthday is on a Tuesday.

It is after June 22.

Brianna's birthday is _____.

June Birthdays

June						
Sun.	Mon.	Tues.	Wed.	Thurs.	Fri.	Sat.
		1	2	3	4	5
6	7	8	9	10	11	12
13	14	15	16	17	18	19
20	21	22	23	24	25	26
27	28	29	30			

Pavel's birthday is after June 9.

It is before June 21.

It is on a Wednesday.

Pavel's birthday is _____.

June Birthdays

June						
Sun.	Mon.	Tues.	Wed.	Thurs.	Fri.	Sat.
		1	2	3	4	5
6	7	8	9	10	11	12
13	14	15	16	17	18	19
20	21	22	23	24	25	26
27	28	29	30			

Madison's birthday is on a day that starts with *T.*

It is before June 29.

It is after June 17.

It is not June 22.

Madison's birthday is _____.

What Did You Buy?

Standards

- Adds and subtracts whole numbers
- Solves real-world problems involving addition and subtraction of whole numbers

Overview

Students use information to find a total number of objects or specific items purchased.

Problem-Solving Strategies

- Count, compute, or write an equation
- Find information in a picture, list, table, graph, or diagram
- Guess and check or make an estimate

Materials

- *What Did You Buy?* (page 85; whatbuy.pdf)
- classroom calendar
- sticky notes (*optional*)
- *Student Response Form* (page 130; studentresponse.pdf) (*optional*)

Activate

1. Sketch a large bag labeled *10 balloons*, a medium bag labeled *8 balloons* and a small bag labeled *6 balloons*. Ask *If you buy two small bags of balloons, how many balloons will you buy? How did you find the answer? What equation could you write to show this? What if you bought 20 balloons?*

2. Ask students how you can buy 16 balloons. Ask for volunteers with other solutions.

Solve

1. Distribute copies of *What Did You Buy?* to students. Have students work alone, in pairs, or in small groups.

2. Before debriefing, you may want to have students place their work on their desks and take a walk to see how others recorded their thinking. As students take this gallery walk listen to their comments to learn what they notice and what connections they make.

3. Provide feedback such as *You made several guesses without giving up.*

Debrief

1. What answer did you find?

2. What strategies did you use?

3. How did making a guess help you?

Differentiate ▢ △

Students solving the on-level and above-level problems may be helped by writing the numbers on sticky notes that they can move together to check their sums.

What Did You Buy?

| Monster Erasers: 12 |
| Princess Erasers: 1 |

You buy these erasers.

How many erasers did you buy?

What Did You Buy?

| Pirate Coins: 23 |
| Pirate Prizes: 9 |
| Pirate Treasures: 7 |

You buy 30 pirate goodies.

Which two boxes of pirate goodies did you buy?

What Did You Buy?

| Note Cards: 13 |
| Thank-You Cards: 14 |
| Birthday Cards: 9 |
| Get Well Cards: 8 |

You buy 22 cards.

Which two boxes of cards did you buy?

Tell another way you could do it.

Ring Toss

Standards

- Understands symbolic, concrete, and pictorial representations of numbers
- Uses base-ten concepts to compare and represent whole numbers in flexible ways
- Adds and subtracts whole numbers

Overview

A ring toss board is pictured in which tosses can score 10 points or 1 point. Rings have landed on the board and students determine the total value of the tosses. Then, they answer an additional question after another toss scores points.

Problem-Solving Strategies

- Count, compute, or write an equation
- Find information in a picture, list, table, graph, or diagram
- Organize information in a picture, list, table, graph, or diagram

Materials

- *Ring Toss* (page 87; ringtoss.pdf)
- *Ring Toss Template* (ringtosstemplate.pdf)
- *Student Response Form* (page 130; studentresponse.pdf) *(optional)*

Activate

1. Ask students if they have ever played a ring toss game. Provide time for a few students who have done so to describe the game and tell where they played it. Alternatively, you could have a student dramatize playing the game and have the other students guess the game the student was demonstrating.

2. Display the *Ring Toss Template* for students. Ask *If I tossed three rings and got three points, where did the rings land? What if I got 12 points? What if I got 30 points?*

Solve

1. Distribute copies of *Ring Toss* to students. Have students work alone or in pairs. Have students note the boards and tosses that have already been made.

Debrief

1. How did you find the total points for the rings shown? Did anyone find the total in a different way?

2. How did you find the total after the player got more points? Did anyone find the total in a different way?

3. How might someone use a drawing to find this total?

Differentiate ⬤

For students who would benefit from more experience with finding the total points shown, you can draw rings on the *Ring Toss Template* and have students write the corresponding numbers. If possible, make an actual ring toss game that students can play for additional practice.

Ring Toss ○

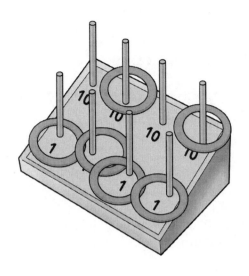

Jessie tossed these rings.

How many points does Jessie have?

Then, he gets another 10 points.

How many points does Jessie have now?

Ring Toss ▢

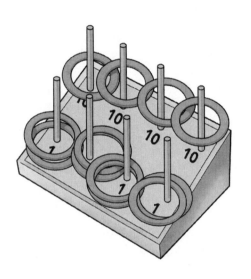

Kareem tossed these rings.

How many points does Kareem have?

Then, he gets 20 more points.

How many points does Kareem have now?

Ring Toss △

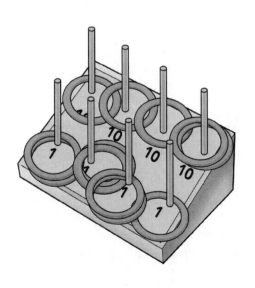

Simone tossed six more rings.

Some of these rings scored points.

Now Simone has 70 points.

How many of these rings got points?

Favorite Numbers

Standard

Adds and subtracts whole numbers

Overview

These problems require students to estimate or add to identify a favorite number from a set of numbers. Then, they find the number that is a given amount less than that number.

Problem-Solving Strategies

- Count, compute, or write an equation
- Find information in a picture, list, table, graph, or diagram
- Use logical reasoning

Materials

- *Favorite Numbers* (page 89; favoritenumbers.pdf)
- individual white boards (*optional*)
- base-ten blocks, hundreds charts, or counters (*optional*)
- *Student Response Form* (page 130; studentresponse.pdf) (*optional*)

Activate

1. Display the numbers 17, 35, and 42. Ask students which number is 30 more than 5 (*35*). Then ask which number is 7 more than 10 (*17*), and which is 10 more than 32 (*42*). If available, have students write the answer on individual white boards and hold them up for you to see. Ask students how they found each number.

2. Repeat step 1 for the numbers 25, 74, and 64. This time ask which number is 10 more than 15 (*25*), which is 50 more than 14 (*64*), and which is 20 more than 54 (*74*). Have students share their reasoning.

3. Ask students what the word *favorite* means. Allow a few students to identify a favorite game, food, or sport. Tell students that they are going to solve some problems about favorite numbers.

Solve

1. Distribute copies of *Favorite Numbers* to students. Make sure students understand that the favorite numbers are contained in the boxes. Have students work alone or in pairs.

2. As students work, provide descriptive feedback such as *I see you are checking your answer with the numbers in the box. I notice you counted back to find the number that is less.*

Debrief

1. What strategies did you use to find the favorite number?

2. Who can tell us how they found the number that was less?

3. How might we find 9 less than 20?

4. Could you find the answer without the numbers in the box?

Differentiate ⭕ ⬜ △ ☆

Some students may wish to pose problems based on their own favorite numbers. Encourage them to do so. For those students who are less comfortable working at an abstract level, have them model the problems using base-ten blocks, counters, or hundreds charts.

Favorite Numbers

Choose your answer from the box below.

| 32 | 50 | 60 |

My favorite number is 10 more than 40.

What is 10 more than my favorite number?

Favorite Numbers

Choose your answer from the box below.

| 58 | 38 | 48 |

My favorite number is 18 more than 20.

What is 20 more than my favorite number?

Favorite Numbers

Choose your answer from the box below.

| 72 | 52 | 82 |

My favorite number is 20 more than 62.

What is 30 less than my favorite number?

What Is the Number?

Standards

- Understands symbolic, concrete, and pictorial representations of numbers
- Uses base-ten concepts to compare and represent whole numbers in flexible ways

Overview

Students are shown pictures with different quantities of tens and ones blocks, use clues to identify the correct representation, and write the number in standard form.

Problem-Solving Strategies

- Count, compute, or write an equation
- Find information in a picture, list, table, graph, or diagram
- Use logical reasoning

Materials

- *What Is the Number?* (page 91; whatnumber.pdf)
- base-ten blocks (tens and ones)
- *Student Response Form* (page 130; studentresponse.pdf) *(optional)*

Activate

1. Display the numbers 24 and 32 using base-ten blocks. Have students identify the numbers represented.

2. Have each student silently pick one of the numbers. Then ask them which clue they can tell the class so that others would know which number they picked. Have a student share his or her clue and have other students name the number. Invite other students to share different clues for this same number.

3. Direct students' attention to the other number. Have students share original ideas for clues and then brainstorm more clues for this number.

Solve

1. Distribute copies of *What Is the Number?* to students. Explain that this time they will use more than just one clue to identify the number. Have students work alone, in pairs, or in small groups.

2. Listen as students work. Do they refer to tens and ones? Do they use correct number names?

Debrief

1. Give an example of how you used a clue to eliminate a number.

2. What is a different clue we can create to eliminate the same number?

3. What did you do to help you remember that a number had been eliminated?

Differentiate ◯ ☆

Some students may benefit from exploring the process of elimination within a non-numerical context prior to this activity. For example, dramatize a family deciding what vegetable to have for dinner and one child says, "I don't like peas." Talk about *eliminating* peas as a choice.

What Is the Number?

Jake used base-ten blocks to show a number.

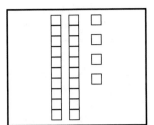 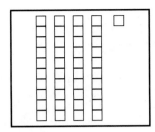 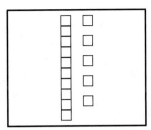

Jake used more than one ten to show his number.

Jake's number is less than 35.

Circle Jake's number.

Write Jake's number. _____

What Is the Number?

Amanda used base-ten blocks to show a number.

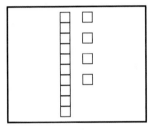 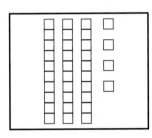 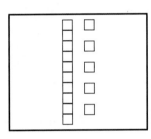 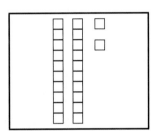

Amanda's number is less than 30.

Amanda used more ones than tens to show her number.

Her number is not equal to 10 + 5.

Circle Amanda's number. Write Amanda's number. _____

What Is the Number?

Owen used base-ten blocks to show a number.

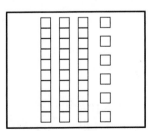 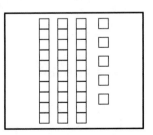 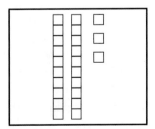 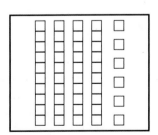

Owen's number is greater than 30.

With four more units, Owen would need to trade ones for a ten.

Owen's number is not equal to 40 + 6.

Circle Owen's number. Write Owen's number. _____

Number Groups

Standards

- Uses base-ten concepts to compare and represent whole numbers in flexible ways
- Recognizes regularities in a variety of contexts

Overview

In this problem set, students are given a group of four numbers and consider similarities and differences among them. They are asked to pick one number and tell how it is different. These problems encourage students to refer to the tens and ones places as well as to compare numbers.

Problem-Solving Strategies

- Find information in a picture, list, table, graph, or diagram
- Generalize a pattern

Materials

- *Number Groups* (page 93; numbergroups.pdf)
- *Student Response Form* (page 130; studentresponse.pdf) *(optional)*

Activate

1. Display the numbers 23, 21, 5, and 26. Ask students to work in pairs or small groups to choose a number that is different from the others and to explain their thinking. Encourage them to find more than one way in which their number is different. Most students will choose the number five and explain that it is not in the twenties, is less than 10, or is the only number that does not have a 2 before it. Some students familiar with odd and even numbers will choose 26 and state that it is the only even number.

Solve

1. Distribute copies of *Number Groups* to students. Have students work in pairs or in small groups so they can share their thinking and various ways of explaining the differences.

2. Engage students by asking *If you were going to pick one of these numbers for a sports shirt, which one would you pick? Why?*

3. Provide descriptive feedback, such as *I see you listen carefully to your partner's ideas. I hear you using mathematical terms correctly.*

Debrief

1. What number do you think is different? Why do you think so?

2. Is there another way to explain how it is different?

3. Does anyone think another number is different? How is it different?

Differentiate ⬤ ◼ △ ☆

Students who like to find similarities and differences may wish to create their own sets of four numbers and challenge others to find the number that is different. Some students may be able to solve the above-level problem if they only need to identify one number that is different.

Number Groups

Choose a number from the box. How is it different from all the other numbers? Explain why it is different.

6	8	15	1

Number Groups

Choose a number from the box. How is it different from all the other numbers? Explain why it is different.

10	61	30	50

Number Groups

Choose a number from the box. How is it different from all the other numbers? Explain why it is different.

2	14	17	30

Choose another number from the box. How is it different from all the other numbers? Explain why it is different.

How Long?

Standard
Knows processes for measuring length

Overview
Students are given information about the lengths of three items. They use statements with the comparative terms of *shorter*, *longer*, *shortest*, and *longest* to determine the color of each item.

Problem-Solving Strategies
- Find information in a picture, list, table, graph, or diagram
- Use logical reasoning

Materials
- *How Long?* (page 95; howlong.pdf)
- 3 different colored crayons of different lengths
- *Student Response Form* (page 130; studentresponse.pdf) *(optional)*

Activate
1. Show students two of the crayons and ask them what they can tell you about them. If no one brings up their different lengths, do so. Ask a volunteer to describe something about the lengths of these two crayons. Have several students explain their reasoning.

2. Display all three crayons. Point to the shortest crayon and ask students what they can say about its length. Repeat, pointing to the longest and then to the middle crayon.

3. Repeat with three other crayons, if necessary, to ensure that all students are familiar with the comparative terms *shorter/shortest* and *longer/longest*.

Solve
1. Distribute copies of *How Long?* to students. Have students work alone, in pairs, or in small groups.

2. As students are working, ask questions such as *How do you decide which one is longer?*

Debrief
1. How did you know how to label the items?

2. Is there another way we could write one of the clues?

Differentiate ◯ ◻ △ ☆
Have English language learners create a picture dictionary of the comparative terms. If you wish to gather formative assessment data to inform further instructional plans, assign an exit card task such as: *Draw a picture of two lines that have different lengths. Circle the line that is longer.* Or, if your students are comfortable writing, have them write a sentence about the lines using the word *longer*.

How Long? ○

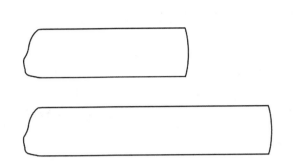

The blue chalk is shorter.

The yellow chalk is longer.

Color the chalk.

How Long? ☐

The green crayon is the longest.

The yellow crayon is shorter than the red crayon.

Color the crayons.

How Long? ◁

The yellow pencil is the shortest.

The blue pencil is longer than the red pencil.

The green pencil is the longest.

Color the pencils.

Find It

Standards

- Knows processes for measuring length using basic nonstandard units
- Makes quantitative estimates of familiar dimensions and checks them against measurements

Overview

In this problem set, a small paper clip is identified as having a length of 1 unit. Students use this information and problem data to identify or draw a line of a specified length.

Problem-Solving Strategies

- Act it out or use manipulatives
- Find information in a picture, list, table, graph, or diagram
- Guess and check or make an estimate

Materials

- *Find It* (page 97; findit.pdf)
- 6–10 small paper clips per student pair
- *Student Response Form* (page 130; studentresponse.pdf) *(optional)*

Activate

1. Ask students to show you with their hands how long they think a small paper clip is. Note those students who make a reasonable estimate and those who do not. Also observe how they indicate their length. For example, do they show a distance between two fingers or indicate a length along one finger? This information may guide you in how to best work with individual students.

2. Distribute paper clips to students and ask them to place two of the clips end-to-end. Ask *If one paper clip has a length of 1 unit, what is the total length of these paper clips? What will be the length if we add another paper clip?*

Solve

1. Distribute copies of *Find It* to students. Have students work in pairs or in small groups so that they can check with one another, but make sure each student makes his or her own measurement before conferring with others.

2. Observe students as they work. Are they careful to place the paper clips end-to-end without overlapping or leaving gaps?

Debrief

1. How did you find your answer?

2. Did anyone use another strategy?

3. What should you think about when you measure?

Differentiate ○ □ △ ☆

Students may measure in different ways. Some students may prefer to place multiple paper clips beneath a line to measure it. Others may prefer to place one paper clip, mark its end, and then move that same paper clip to the next space. Encourage students to share their different approaches.

Find It ○

A small paper clip has a length of 1 unit.

Nancy measures her crayon. It is three units long.

Which line is the same length as Nancy's crayon? Circle it.

Find It ▢

A small paper clip has a length of 1 unit.

Jason measures the length of his glue stick. It is 2 units longer than Chang's glue stick. Chang's glue stick is two units long.

Which line is the same length as Jason's glue stick? Circle it.

Find It △

A small paper clip has a length of 1 unit.

Kolinda measures her pencil. It is 12 units long. Magda's pencil is 6 units shorter than Kolinda's pencil.

Draw a line as long as Magda's pencil.

Rod Lengths

Standards

- Knows processes for measuring length, weight, and temperature using basic nonstandard units
- Makes quantitative estimates of familiar dimensions and checks them against measurements

Overview

In this problem set, different Cuisenaire rods are assigned a length in units and students use that information to estimate and then measure the lengths of another rod or combination of rods.

Problem-Solving Strategies

- Act it out or use manipulatives
- Count, compute, or write an equation
- Find information in a picture, list, table, graph, or diagram

Materials

- *Rod Lengths* (page 99; rodlengths.pdf)
- Cuisenaire rods
- *Student Response Form* (page 130; studentresponse.pdf) *(optional)*

Activate

1. Distribute Cuisenaire rods to pairs of students. If students have not used the rods before, provide some free exploration time. Many students will build a staircase (one rod of each color, side-by side, organized according to length), but if they do not, encourage them to do so. Then give directions such as *Show me the dark green rod. Show me a rod longer than the yellow one. Show me a rod shorter than the light green one.*

2. Have students hold a red rod in one hand and a dark green rod in the other. Ask *Which color rod is longer? Which is shorter? How many red rods would it take to build a rod as long as the dark green? Make an estimate and then check.* Once everyone agrees it would take three red rods, ask *So if the red is one unit long, how many units long is the dark green rod? How many units long do you think the purple rod would be?*

Solve

1. Distribute copies of *Rod Lengths* to students. Have students work alone, in pairs, or in small groups. Make sure students estimate first and then use the rods to check.

2. Encourage explicit attention to estimation by asking *How did you estimate the number of units?*

Debrief

1. What lengths did you find?

2. What did you learn about your ability to make estimates?

Differentiate ⬭ ▢ △ ☆

Some students may find it difficult not to correct their estimates once they know the real lengths. Help them realize that an estimate does not have to be exact and that estimating helps us better understand measurement.

Rod Lengths ◯

Estimate and then check.

| light green | is 1 unit long.

How long is | dark green | ?

Estimate and then check.

Estimate _____ units

Measure _____ units

Rod Lengths ▢

Estimate and then check.

| purple | is 1 unit long.

How long is

| brown | brown | ?

Estimate and then check.

Estimate _____ units

Measure _____ units

Rod Lengths ◁

Estimate and then check.

| red | is 1 unit long.

How long is | orange | ?

Estimate and then check.

Estimate _____ units

Measure _____ units

What Time?

Standards

- Understands the concept of time and how it is measured
- Knows processes for telling time

Overview

Students are shown clocks and given information about an event. They identify the clock that shows the time of the event or write the time of the event.

Problem-Solving Strategies

- Act it out or use manipulatives
- Use logical reasoning

Materials

- *What Time?* (page 101; whattime.pdf)
- analog clocks (real or play)
- *Student Response Form* (page 130; studentresponse.pdf) *(optional)*

Activate

1. Ask students how the hands of the clock look when it is 3:00. Have several volunteers share responses.

2. Demonstrate the times on an analog clock as you tell this story: *Mrs. Mendez gets up every morning at 6:00.* (Show the clock at 6:00.) *She brushes her teeth, plays with the baby, and gets food ready for breakfast. Then she wakes up the other children at 7:00.* (Move the hour hand to this time.) *These children take showers, get dressed, and eat breakfast. They get on the school bus at 8:30.* (Move the clock's hands to show 8:30.)

3. Distribute analog clocks to students. Retell the story from step 2, but this time have students show the times on their clocks.

Solve

1. Distribute copies of *What Time?* to students. Have students work alone or in pairs.

2. Ask refocusing questions as students work, such as *What number does the shorter hand point to? What does the longer hand tell you?*

Debrief

1. How did you decide the time?

2. If the time is four-thirty, where is the longer hand of the clock? Where is the shorter hand?

3. Which kind of clock do you like best for telling the time? Why?

Differentiate ◯ ▢ △ ☆

For students who need extra practice telling time to the hour, tape the minute hand in place at 12 on a play clock. In pairs, have them move the hour hand and tell the time. Consider assigning an exit card task such as the following: *The long hand is pointing to the twelve. The short hand is pointing to the eleven. What time is it?*

What Time? ◯

Ben has a friend over at 1:00.

Which clock shows the time?

Circle the clock.

What Time? ☐

The clock shows the time that Jia Li wakes up.

What time does Jia Li wake up?

What Time? △

One of these clocks shows the time Mac gets home.

Mac does not get home at 5:30.

Mac does not get home at six-thirty.

What time does Mac get home?

What Happens?

Standards

- Understands the concept of time and how it is measured
- Knows processes for telling time

Overview

In this problem set, students are given information about three events that happen and match them to times shown on a digital or analog clock.

Problem-Solving Strategy

Use logical reasoning

Materials

- *What Happens?* (page 103; whathappens.pdf)
- digital clock (real or play)
- analog clock (real or play)
- *Student Response Form* (page 130; studentresponse.pdf) *(optional)*

Activate

1. Show students a digital clock set to 10:00. Have a volunteer name the time while you record it as *10:00* and *ten o'clock*. Ask students to identify things that might happen at this time of the morning.

2. Show students an analog clock set to 12:00. Ask students what time the clock shows. Ask if there is another name for this time of day *(noon)* or night *(midnight)*.

3. Set the digital clock to show 1:30 and have the students tell the time shown. Record *1:30* and *one-thirty*. Have another student show the same time on the analog clock. Ask students why some people might call this time *half-past one*.

Solve

1. Distribute copies of *What Happens?* to students. Have students work in pairs or in small groups to encourage discussions of their thinking. Point out the words in bold and make sure students understand that they should write these words under the correct clocks.

2. Listen to students as they work. Do they say *nine-thirty* or *half-past nine*?

Debrief

1. Who can tell us how to find an answer?

2. Which clue did you use first?

3. How else could you solve this problem?

Differentiate ○ □ △ ☆

Have both analog and digital clocks available for use so that students may refer to both models as they wish. Digital clocks do not help students understand why we might refer to nine-thirty as half past nine, yet some students may come from homes where this expression is used. Knowing which terms students use will help you better meet their needs.

What Happens?

Write words under each clock to show what happens when.

The Lee family comes **home** at 6:00.

They eat **dinner** at 7:00.

Gavin goes to **bed** at eight o'clock.

What Happens?

Write words under each clock to show what happens when.

Rory has **lunch** at noon.

She goes to her **grandma's house** at three o'clock.

She goes **home** at 5:30.

What Happens?

Write words under each clock to show what happens when.

Evan **gets up** at 6:30 on Saturday.

He has a soccer **game** at nine-thirty.

He eats **breakfast** two hours before the game.

Finding Favorites

Standards

- Counts whole numbers
- Solves real-world problems involving addition and subtraction of whole numbers
- Collects and represents information about objects or events in simple graphs

Overview

Students respond to questions by finding the appropriate information about favorite sports, pies, and recess games in picture graphs. The information is shown with smiley faces, so counting is emphasized.

Problem-Solving Strategies

- Count, compute, or write an equation
- Find information in a picture, list, table, graph, or diagram

Materials

- *Finding Favorites* (page 105; favorites.pdf)
- *Student Response Form* (page 130; studentresponse.pdf) *(optional)*

Activate

1. Ask students why they might want to know about the class's favorite game or book.

2. Create a blank pictograph on the board. Write the names of three classroom games in the first column. Invite each student to draw a smiley face in the appropriate row to indicate their favorite game.

3. Ask students how we could use this graph to find how many students chose a certain game as their favorite. Ask *How might this information be helpful to us?*

Solve

1. Distribute copies of *Finding Favorites* to students. Tell them that these graphs show information about other classes' favorites. Have students work alone, in pairs, or in small groups to find answers. When working together, all students should count the smiley faces to ensure accuracy.

2. As you observe students at work listen to hear if students are using comparative words such as *more* or *most* and *fewer* and *fewest* appropriately.

Debrief

1. How does the word *not* tell you what to count?

2. What did you do to help you keep track of the smiley faces when you counted them? What else could you do to help you keep track?

Differentiate ◯

As they count, some students may find it helpful to write the numbers 1, 2, 3, 4, and so forth, directly on the smiley faces.

Favorite Sport   ☺ = 1 child

baseball	☺ ☺ ☺ ☺ ☺ ☺ ☺ ☺
basketball	☺ ☺ ☺ ☺
soccer	☺ ☺ ☺ ☺ ☺ ☺

How many children chose soccer?

Favorite Pie   ☺ = 1 child

apple	☺ ☺ ☺ ☺ ☺ ☺ ☺
blueberry	☺ ☺ ☺ ☺ ☺ ☺ ☺ ☺
chocolate	☺ ☺ ☺ ☺ ☺ ☺ ☺

How many children did not choose apple pie?

Favorite Recess Games   ☺ = 1 child

keep away	☺ ☺ ☺ ☺ ☺ ☺ ☺ ☺ ☺
kickball	☺ ☺ ☺ ☺ ☺ ☺ ☺ ☺
tag	☺ ☺ ☺ ☺ ☺ ☺

How many children chose a favorite game?

Make a Graph

Standards

- Understands that numerals are symbols used to represent quantities or attributes of real-world objects
- Counts whole numbers
- Solves real-world problems involving addition and subtraction of whole numbers
- Collects and represents information about objects or events in simple graphs

Overview

Students are shown pictures of sets (grouped and not grouped) and draw the bars in a graph to show the number in each set.

Problem-Solving Strategies

- Count, compute, or write an equation
- Find information in a picture, list, table, graph, or diagram
- Organize information in a picture, list, table, graph, or diagram

Materials

- *Make a Graph* (page 107; makegraph.pdf)
- *Flower Picture and Graph* (flowers.pdf)
- *Student Response Form* (page 130; studentresponse.pdf) *(optional)*

Activate

1. Show students the *Flower Picture and Graph* and have them identify the roses, daisies, and tulips. Ask *How many roses are there? How can we use the pictures to find the answer? How can we use the graph to find the answer? Is one way easier than the other?*

2. Repeat step 1, asking whether there are more daisies or tulips.

Solve

1. Distribute copies of *Make a Graph* to students. Have students work alone, in pairs, or in small groups. Point out that students are to make bars to show the number of objects and then answer the question. Each student should make his or her own graph.

2. If students are working with others, note how actively involved each student is and whether the student is making suggestions or following what other students say to do.

Debrief

1. Who can show us a way to use counting to find an answer?

2. Who can show us how to use the graph to find an answer?

3. Why do you think we show information in graphs?

Differentiate ◉

Some students may have difficulty keeping track of the count when the objects are not grouped in an orderly way. Students may wish to cross off a picture to show it has been counted.

Number of Fruits

Fruits

	1	2	3	4	5	6	7
bananas							
apples							
oranges							

Are there more bananas or apples?

Number of Toys

Toys

	1	2	3	4	5	6	7	8
cars								
bears								
trucks								

How many toys have wheels?

Number of Animals

Animals

	1	2	3	4	5	6	7	8	9
birds									
frogs									
rabbits									
worms									

How many animals are there in all?

Make a Graph ○

Make a Graph □

Make a Graph △

Point Totals

Standards

- Adds and subtracts whole numbers
- Solves real-world problems involving addition and subtraction of whole numbers
- Collects and represents information about objects or events in simple graphs

Overview

Students are shown line plots that show the points scored by three players. They use the information in the graph to answer questions about the point totals that involve finding sums and differences.

Problem-Solving Strategies

- Count, compute, or write an equation
- Find information in a picture, list, table, graph, or diagram

Materials

- *Point Totals* (page 109; pointtotals.pdf)
- connecting cubes
- *Student Response Form* (page 130; studentresponse.pdf) *(optional)*

Activate

1. Ask students what they think the score keeper does when teams play games.

2. Ask students what games they play in which they score points. Encourage students to think about different categories of games, for example, sports, video games, and card games.

3. Say *Imagine three friends were playing a game. After the game ended they made a graph to show their points. How might we tell who won by looking at their graph?*

Solve

1. Distribute copies of *Point Totals* to students. Have students work alone or in pairs. Explain to them that all of the questions are about the same graph. Ask *What is this graph about? Who do you think scored the most points? Why do you think so?* Repeat, asking about the player who scored the fewest number of points.

2. As students work, ask them questions about what they are thinking as they answer each question or how they could prove their answer is correct.

Debrief

1. How many points did Tisa score? How do you know?

2. What did you get for an answer? How did you find it?

3. Is there another way to use the graph to find the answer?

Differentiate 🔘

Some students may find it challenging to count the number of Xs. You may want to help a small group of students make cube towers to represent each set of points. Placing the towers side-by-side can help students determine the differences. Alternatively, encourage some students to count the Xs in each column and record the number. Have an identified *checker* confirm the totals before they proceed.

Point Totals ○

Points Scored

```
x
x
x
x              x
x       x      x
x       x      x
x       x      x
x       x      x
x       x      x
x       x      x
_____
Yu     Louis   Tisa
       Player
```

How many more points did
Yu score than Tisa?

Point Totals ▢

Points Scored

```
x
x
x
x              x
x       x      x
x       x      x
x       x      x
x       x      x
x       x      x
x       x      x
_____
Yu     Louis   Tisa
       Player
```

How many points did Louis
and Tisa score together?

Point Totals ◁

Points Scored

```
x
x
x
x              x
x       x      x
x       x      x
x       x      x
x       x      x
x       x      x
x       x      x
_____
Yu     Louis   Tisa
       Player
```

If Yu scores 3 more points
and Tisa scores 8 more
points, who will have more
points? How many more?

What Do We Know?

Standards

- Solves real-world problems involving addition and subtraction of whole numbers
- Collects and represents information about objects or events in simple graphs

Overview

Students are shown a picture graph about a collection of objects. They pose a question that can be answered by using the information in the graph.

Problem-Solving Strategies

- Count, compute, or write an equation
- Find information in a picture, list, table, graph, or diagram

Materials

- *What Do We Know?* (page 111; whatdoweknow.pdf)
- *Student Response Form* (page 130; studentresponse.pdf) *(optional)*

Activate

1. Sketch the pictograph below on the board. Ask students what the graph shows.

Utensils

forks	🍴🍴🍴🍴🍴🍴🍴
knives	🔪🔪🔪🔪🔪🔪🔪🔪
spoons	🥄🥄🥄🥄🥄🥄🥄🥄🥄🥄

2. Ask students what questions they can ask that can be answered using the information in this graph. Direct students to think for a minute on their own and then share ideas with a partner. Tell the pairs to record at least two different questions.

3. Have the pairs share their questions. Help students think about different types of questions. Ask *Does anyone have a question similar to this one? Does anyone have a different question?*

4. There are a variety of questions that students might pose. They might ask about the number in a particular group or about the total number. They might ask questions that compare one group to another or questions that include new data such as *If two people each take a spoon out of the drawer, how many spoons are left?*

Solve

1. Distribute copies of *What Do We Know?* to students. Have students work alone or in pairs.

2. Encourage students completing more than one problem to vary their questions.

Debrief

1. What question did you ask? What answer did you get?

2. Who made up a question that is similar? Different?

Differentiate ☆

Pair students who may be challenged by recording their work with an English-proficient partner.

In the Cookie Jar

chocolate chip	🍪 🍪 🍪 🍪 🍪 🍪 🍪 🍪 🍪
gingerbread	🧍 🧍 🧍 🧍
peanut butter	🥔 🥔

Write a question that you can answer by using this graph. Use **chocolate chip** in your question.

In the Parking Lot

cars	🚗 🚗 🚗 🚗 🚗 🚗 🚗 🚗 🚗 🚗 🚗 🚗 🚗 🚗
trucks	🛻 🛻 🛻 🛻 🛻
vans	🚐 🚐 🚐 🚐 🚐 🚐 🚐

Make up a question about what is in the parking lot. Use the word **more** in your question.

In the Shape Box

circles	● ● ● ● ● ● ● ●
squares	■ ■ ■ ■ ■ ■ ■ ■ ■ ■ ■ ■ ■
triangles	▲ ▲ ▲ ▲ ▲ ▲ ▲ ▲ ▲

Make up a question about the shapes in the box. Show how addition could be used to answer your question.

First Names

Standards

- Collects and represents information about objects or events in simple graphs
- Understands that one can find out about a group of things by studying just a few of them
- Understands that some events are more likely to happen than others

Overview

Given a list, students examine characteristics of their classmates' first names. They count according to the given criteria and make tally marks in a graph to summarize the information.

Problem-Solving Strategies

- Count, compute, or write an equation
- Organize information in a picture, list, table, graph, or diagram

Materials

- *First Names* (page 113; firstnames.pdf)
- class list of students' first names
- *Student Response Form* (page 130; studentresponse.pdf) *(optional)*

Activate

1. Display a list of students' first names for the class. Read the names aloud. Ask questions such as *Whose first name begins with the letter B?* Model making a tally mark for each name as it is read. Ask students how many names begin with the letter *B*.

2. Have students identify the first five names on the list. Ask *Which of these names have the letter a in them?* Again, model making tally marks as each name is read. Ask how many names have the letter *a* in them.

Solve

1. Distribute copies of *First Names* to students. Have students work in pairs so one student can identify the names as the other makes tally marks. Explain that they will be finding information about the first names in their class.

2. Encourage students to exchange roles and repeat the task to check for accuracy.

Debrief

1. What did you find out about the first names in our class?

2. Do you think that most of the first names in the class next door end in *y*? Why or why not?

3. Do you think there are fewer than five first names in the class next door with the letter *e*? Why do you think so?

Differentiate

If the list of names is too long for some of your students to consider, cut the list in half. Students interested in a challenge may want to compare the data of your class and another class. Provide them with a list and have students collect the same data. Encourage them to compare the results for both classes.

First Names

Names That End with *y*

Yes	
No	

Look at the first name of each classmate.

Does it end in *y*?

Write tally marks in the chart.

How many names end in *y*?

First Names

First Names With e

No	
Exactly 1 *e*	
More than 1 *e*	

Look at the first name of each classmate.

Does it have an *e* in it?

Does it have more than one *e* in it?

Write tally marks in the chart.

How many of the names have one or more *e*?

First Names

Letters in First Name

Less than 8	
Exactly 8	
More than 8	

Look at the first name of each classmate.

How many letters are in the name?

Are there more, less, or exactly 8 letters?

Write tally marks in the chart.

Do most of the names have 8 or more letters? Explain.

What Shape Is Next?

Standards

- Uses the names of simple geometric shapes to represent and describe real-world situations
- Extends simple patterns

Overview

Students are shown geometric patterns and asked to draw the next shape in the pattern and then to write the name of the shape.

Problem-Solving Strategies

- Act it out or use manipulatives
- Generalize a pattern

Materials

- *What Shape Is Next?* (page 115; whatshape.pdf)
- squares, circles, triangles such as those found in attribute sets
- *Student Response Form* (page 130; studentresponse.pdf) *(optional)*

Activate

1. Distribute attribute blocks to students. If they have not used the materials recently provide some time for free exploration.

2. Have students make a row of blocks in this order: triangle, square, triangle, square, triangle, square. Ask *What shape is next? How do you know? What unit repeats?*

3. Repeat step 2 with the following sequence: square, square, circle, square, square, circle, square, square, circle, square.

Solve

1. Distribute copies of *What Shape Is Next?* to students. Have students work alone, in pairs, or in small groups. Make the blocks available for those students who would benefit from building the patterns.

2. Observe students as they work. Do they build the pattern? Do they say the names of the shapes aloud to help them recognize the pattern?

Debrief

1. What shape comes next?

2. How do you know?

3. What unit is repeated?

4. How could you use different shapes to make the same pattern?

Differentiate ○ ■ △ ☆

You may wish to allow some students to only draw the shape or write its name instead of doing both. Have each student complete an exit card if you wish to gather formative assessment data for making further instructional plans. Give each student a small card and have them create their own shape pattern on it. Note their drawings of the shapes as well as the complexity of their patterns.

What Shape Is Next?

Draw the next shape.

☐ ◯ ☐ ◯ ☐ ◯ ☐ _____

What is the name of the shape?

What Shape Is Next?

Draw the next shape.

△ ◯ ☐ △ ◯ ☐ △ ◯ ☐ _____

What is the name of the shape?

What Shape Is Next?

Draw the next shape.

☐ △ ☐ ☐ △ ☐ ☐ △ ☐ ☐ △ _____

What is the name of the shape?

What Shape Am I?

Standards

- Understands basic properties of simple geometric shapes and similarities and differences between simple geometric shapes
- Uses the names of simple geometric shapes to represent and describe real-world situations

Overview

Students are given pictures of shapes and clues about one of the shapes. The students use the clues to identify one of the shapes.

Problem-Solving Strategy

Use logical reasoning

Materials

- *What Shape Am I?* (page 117; shapeam.pdf)
- *Student Response Form* (page 130; studentresponse.pdf) *(optional)*

Activate

1. Ask students what they can tell you about a triangle.

2. Draw a picture of a triangle, square, and a rectangle. Tell students that you are thinking of one of these shapes and that you will give them clues to help them determine which one it is. Tell them that the figure has four sides. Have students tell what they know about your shape from the clue. Model crossing off the triangle to show that it is no longer a possibility. Then, say *All of my sides have the same length.* Again, have students tell you what they know and model crossing off the rectangle. Emphasize the importance of checking their thinking. Say *Let's check the square with the two clues. Does it have four sides? Do each of its sides have the same length?*

Solve

1. Distribute copies of *What Shape Am I?* to students. Have students work alone or in pairs.

2. As students work ask them to identify each shape in the problem. Listen to the language they use to describe the figures that are not in traditional positions. For example, rather than a *triangle*, some students refer to an *upside-down triangle* when the base is not parallel to the bottom of the page. In the third problem, how do they talk about the pentagon or trapezoid?

Debrief

1. Which shape did you identify?

2. How did you keep track of what you learned from the clues?

3. How did you check your work?

Differentiate ⬤ ▢ △ ☆

Whenever possible, pair readers who will need some help with those who are more independent in their reading. You may want some emerging readers to work with you in a small group so that you can help them read the clues.

What Shape Am I?

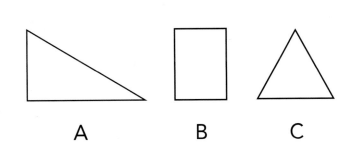

I have three sides.

All of my sides have the same length.

What shape am I? Write the letter of the shape.

_____

What Shape Am I?

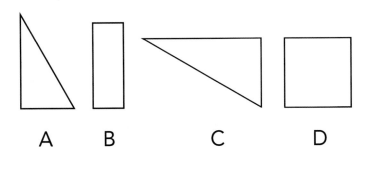

I am not a triangle.

All of my sides are not the same length.

What shape am I? Write the letter of the shape.

_____

What Shape Am I?

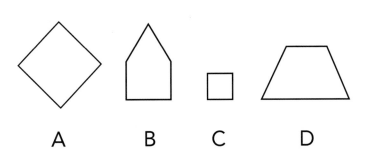

I have four sides.

I am not a square.

What shape am I? Write the letter of the shape.

_____

Build a Design

Standards

- Adds and subtracts whole numbers
- Understands that patterns can be made by putting different shapes together or taking them apart

Overview

In this problem set, students find the total number of points that make up a geometric design based on the number of points assigned for the individual shapes. Students may count or add to find the totals.

Problem-Solving Strategies

- Count, compute, or write an equation
- Find information in a picture, list, table, graph, or diagram

Materials

- *Build a Design* (page 119; builddesign.pdf)
- pattern blocks
- *Student Response Form* (page 130; studentresponse.pdf) *(optional)*

Activate

1. Provide students with pattern blocks and allow a few minutes for free design. To review vocabulary, ask students to name the shapes used in their designs.

2. Ask *If you needed 1 point to get a triangle, how many points do you think you need to get this rhombus?* (Hold up the triangle and blue rhombus.) *What about this trapezoid?* Encourage children to use the relationship among the shapes to decide that it would make sense for the rhombus to be worth two points, and the trapezoid three points.

3. Hold up a triangle sharing a side with the trapezoid. Ask students how many points they would need to get this design.

Solve

1. Distribute copies of *Build a Design* to students. Draw their attention to the number of points given in the boxes. Have students work alone, in pairs, or in small groups.

2. Observe students as they work. What strategies do they use to find the total?

Debrief

1. Who used counting to find an answer? Show us.

2. Who used addition to find an answer? Show us.

3. How could solving the first problem help you solve the second one?

Differentiate

Students who lack addition skills but have strong spatial skills are likely to succeed if they build the design with pattern blocks or template pieces and then place triangles on top of the other non-triangular shapes. Students can then count the triangles by ones to find the total points.

How many points is the
figure below worth?

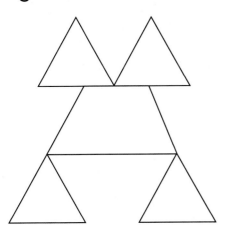

triangle = 1 point

rhombus = 2 points

trapezoid = 3 points

How many points is the
figure below worth?

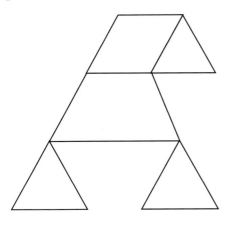

triangle = 1 point

rhombus = 2 points

trapezoid = 3 points

How many points is the
figure below worth?

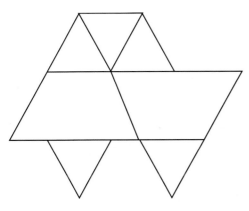

triangle = 1 point

rhombus = 2 points

trapezoid = 3 points

Make It

Standards

- Uses the names of simple geometric shapes to represent and describe real-world situations
- Understands that patterns can be made by putting different shapes together or taking them apart

Overview

Students are shown figures composed of two shapes, a triangle and a square. They decide how many of each shape is needed to make the figure and draw lines to indicate the individual shapes.

Problem-Solving Strategies

- Act it out or use manipulatives
- Count, compute, or write an equation
- Guess and check or make an estimate
- Use logical reasoning

Materials

- *Make It* (page 121; makeit.pdf)
- pattern blocks
- *Student Response Form* (page 130; studentresponse.pdf) *(optional)*

Activate

1. Distribute triangle and square pattern blocks to students. Sketch the figures below:

    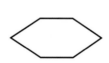

   Tell students that they can make these figures with their pattern blocks. Point to the first figure and ask students how many squares were used to make it. Ask a student to mark the square in the figure. Then ask how many triangles were used.

2. Repeat the same process with the second figure. This time also ask *How could the first figure help us count the triangles and square in the second figure?*

Solve

1. Distribute copies of *Make It* to students. Have students work alone, in pairs, or in small groups.

2. To help some students get started, ask them where the triangles might be needed.

Debrief

1. Who can show us a way to use counting to find an answer?

2. What helped you identify the shapes?

3. How could you explain your ideas to a friend?

Differentiate △

Challenge those students with strong spatial relations to try to decompose the figures into triangles and squares without using the materials.

Make It ○

Write the number to tell how many of each shape you need.

Draw lines to show the shapes.

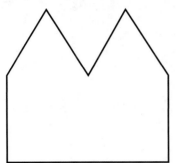   

_____   _____

Make It ▢

Write the number to tell how many of each shape you need.

Draw lines to show the shapes.

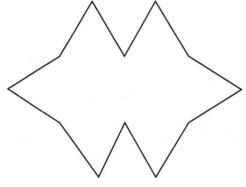   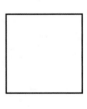

_____   _____

Make It △

Write the number to tell how many of each shape you need.

Draw lines to show the shapes.

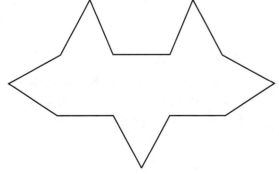 

_____   _____

   121

What Comes Next?

Standards

- Uses the names of simple geometric shapes to represent and describe real-world situations
- Extends simple patterns

Overview

In this problem set, students are given designs made with triangles and squares. Students find patterns among the given examples and use the pattern to predict the number of triangles and squares in a subsequent design.

Problem-Solving Strategies

- Act it out or use manipulatives
- Count, compute, or write an equation
- Generalize a pattern
- Organize information in a picture, list, table, graph, or diagram

Materials

- *What Comes Next?* (page 123; whatnext.pdf)
- pattern blocks
- *Student Response Form* (page 130; studentresponse.pdf) *(optional)*

Activate

1. Tell students that Gina used pattern blocks to make the following pattern:

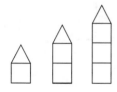

2. Ask students to describe what they see. Encourage several responses.

3. Ask students how Gina's next rocket will look and how many triangles and squares there will be.

4. Use their directions to build the next rocket and ask *How do you know this fits the pattern?*

Solve

1. Distribute copies of *What Comes Next?* to students. Have students work alone, in pairs, or in small groups. Have pattern blocks available for students who wish to build the designs.

2. Support some students by asking *How many squares do you see in this figure?*

Debrief

1. What patterns did you see?

2. What did you do to decide how the next design would look?

Differentiate △

Students ready for a greater challenge may wish to make their own design pattern and share it with a classmate.

Vito builds rows of houses. He follows a pattern.

Vito will use _____ 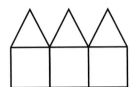 and _____ ☐ in the next row of houses.

Miley builds towers. She follows a pattern.

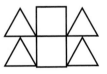 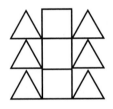 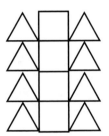

Miley will use _____ △ and _____ ☐ in the next tower.

Zak builds castles. He follows a pattern.

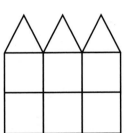 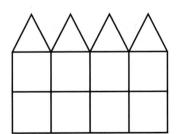 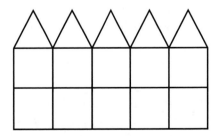

Zak makes more castles. In one castle he uses 10 △.

How many ☐ did Zak use to make that castle?

Shape Creatures

Standards

- Understands basic properties of simple geometric shapes and similarities and differences between simple geometric shapes
- Uses the names of simple geometric shapes to represent and describe real-world situations

Overview

Students are shown examples of creatures that do and do not fit the creature category. Students deduce the features that are necessary and then decide which of three given creatures meets the conditions to be included in the category.

Problem-Solving Strategies

- Find information in a picture, list, table, graph, or diagram
- Generalize a pattern
- Use logical reasoning

Materials

- *Shape Creatures* (page 125; shapecreatures.pdf)
- 3 blue objects and 3 non-blue objects (or other easily identifiable discrete categories)
- *Student Response Form* (page 130; studentresponse.pdf) *(optional)*

Activate

1. Show students three blue objects and tell them that they are going to decide what makes a "blick." Have students identify objects one at a time. When an object is named, say that any blue object is a blick and any non-blue object is not a blick. Ask students what they can tell you about blicks. *(Blicks are blue.)*

Solve

1. Distribute copies of *Shape Creatures* to students. Have students work alone, in pairs, or in small groups. Tell students that the figures on the left fit the rules, while those on the right do not. Make sure students understand that they use this information to decide which one of the following figures also fits the category.

2. As students work, ask *How do you think these creatures look alike? How are they different from the shapes that do not fit?*

Debrief

1. How would you describe a (name of category)?

2. Which figure did you find that fit the rules?

3. How did you decide that it fit the rules?

4. What figure could you draw that would also fit the rules?

Differentiate ◯ ▢ △

Students who are not visual learners may be challenged by information that is presented visually. Have them describe what they see to a partner. The words will help them identify common attributes.

Shape Creatures

These are all rips.	None of these are rips.

Which of these is a rip?

A   B   C

Shape Creatures

These are all blips.	None of these are blips.

Which of these is a blip?

A   B   C

Shape Creatures

These are all trops.	None of these are trops.

Which of these is a trop?

A   B   C

Venn Diagram

Standard

Understands basic properties of simple geometric shapes and similarities and differences between simple geometric shapes

Overview

Students are shown two-ring Venn diagrams and a geometric label for each ring. They then decide where a given shape would be placed in the diagram or draw a shape for an identified portion of the diagram.

Problem-Solving Strategies

- Find information in a picture, list, table, graph, or diagram
- Use logical reasoning

Materials

- *Venn Diagram* (page 127; venn.pdf)
- two 10-ft. pieces of string or yarn, each tied at its ends
- *Student Response Form* (page 130; studentresponse.pdf) *(optional)*

Activate

1. In an open place in the classroom or school, arrange two pieces of string or yarn to make a two-ring Venn diagram on the floor. Create two labels, such as *Wearing Shoes That Tie* and *Has Brown Hair*. Place a label in each ring.

2. Have a student stand beside the first label and have the other students decide whether or not the label is true. Depending on the situation, say *So, (child's name) is in this ring,* or *So, (child's name) is not in this ring.* Repeat for the second label. Then, ask *Where does (child's name) stand?*

3. Repeat until at least one student is in each of the four possible positions in the two-ring diagram (one in each ring, one in the center, one outside the rings). Point out these four places. Repeat with new labels as desired.

Solve

1. Distribute copies of *Venn Diagram* to students. Have students work alone, in pairs, or in small groups. Direct students to use numbers to identify the correct location.

2. Ask refocusing questions such as *How are these shapes the same? How are they different?*

Debrief

1. Where did you put the shape? Why?

2. Can you draw another shape that would go there?

3. What shape did you draw in the third problem? Did anyone draw a different shape?

Differentiate △

Have students draw additional shapes that would fit in each of the other regions.

Venn Diagram ⚪

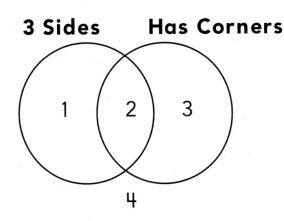

Where does △ go?

Venn Diagram ▢

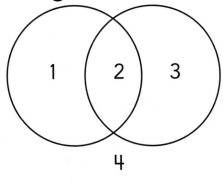

Where does ▭ go?

Venn Diagram ◁

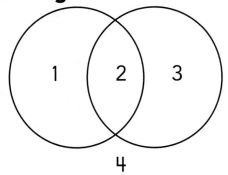

Draw a shape that goes in 4.

Tasty Treats

Standards

- Understands the concept of a unit and its subdivision into equal parts
- Understands that patterns can be made by putting different shapes together or taking them apart

Overview

Students are given a picture of a whole unit and identify the correct picture of the fractional part identified.

Problem-Solving Strategies

- Find information in a picture, list, table, graph, or diagram
- Guess and check or make an estimate

Materials

- *Tasty Treats* (page 129; tastytreats.pdf)
- *Student Response Form* (page 130; studentresponse.pdf) *(optional)*

Activate

1. Have students give examples of times they have shared treats with others.

2. Ask *If you shared a treat with your brother and each of you ate the same amount, how much did each of you eat? If you had different amounts, would it still be half because there were two of you?* To clarify show a picture such as the following:

3. Sketch the drawing below and ask what part of the treat Mike ate. Then, ask students what they could do to prove that Mike ate one-half.

   treat   Mike ate

Solve

1. Distribute copies of *Tasty Treats* to students. Have students work in pairs or in small groups.

2. Have students explain their thinking to each other and note if and how they justify their ideas.

Debrief

1. Which piece was eaten?

2. How do you know?

Differentiate ◓

Encourage students to mark the pieces on the whole. Though only an estimate, it will help students who lack confidence see that the correct number of pieces appears to fit. Some students may need to cut out the fractional pieces, make a guess, and then trace the shape to fill the whole.

Tasty Treats

Mr. Hart made this tasty treat:

Marcus ate half of it.

Which piece did Marcus eat?

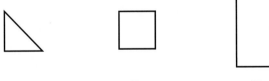

A   B   C

Tasty Treats

Mrs. Stein made this tasty treat:

Bill ate one-fourth of it.

Which piece did Bill eat?

A   B   C

Tasty Treats

Mr. Samson made this tasty treat:

Kim Su ate one-fourth of it.

Which piece did Kim Su eat?

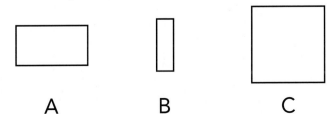

A   B   C

Name: _____   Date: _____

Student Response Form

Problem:

(glue your problem here)

My Work and Illustrations:
(picture, table, list, graph)

My Solution:

My Explanation:

_____

_____

Individual Observation Form

Name: _____ Date: _____

Shows Understanding (Check all that apply.)

☐ Makes representations or notes to understand more fully.

☐ Talks with a peer to understand more fully.

☐ Asks teacher questions to understand more fully.

☐ Interprets problem correctly.

Applies Strategies (Check all that apply.)

☐ Demonstrates use of an appropriate strategy.

☐ Tries an alternative approach when first attempt is unsuccessful.

☐ Uses a strategy appropriately after it is suggested by someone else.

Explains or Justifies Thinking (Check all that apply.)

☐ Communicates thinking clearly.

☐ Uses words and labels to summarize steps to solution.

☐ Provides mathematical justifications for solution or solution process.

☐ Uses correct mathematical vocabulary.

Takes It Further (Check all that apply.)

☐ Makes connections among problems.

☐ Poses new related problems.

☐ Solves a problem in more than one way.

Group Observation Form

Use this form to record scores, comments, or both.

Date: _____

Scores: 1—Beginning   2—Developing   3—Meeting   4—Exceeding

Group Members	Provides leadership/ suggestions to group	Builds on the comments of others	Communicates clearly, uses correct mathematical vocabulary, and builds on the ideas of others	Creates at least one accurate representation of the problem	Suggests/ chooses appropriate strategies					

Record-Keeping Chart

Use this chart to record the problems that were completed. Record the name of the lesson and the date when the appropriate level was completed.

Name: _____

Lesson	⬤ Date Completed	◻ Date Completed	△ Date Completed

Answer Key

At the Farm (page 31)
- 5 horses
- 9 chickens
- ▲ 11 pigs

Stacks of Blocks (page 33)
- 5 blocks
- 11 blocks
- ▲ 7 blocks

Draw and Count (page 35)
- 7 stars
- 3 stars
- ▲ 7, 8, 9, 10, or 11 stars.

Lots of Apples (page 37)
- 7 apples; 5+2=7 or 2+5=7
- 10 apples; 6 + 4 = 10
- ▲ 9 apples; 卌 卌 ||; 3 + 9 = 12

Make It Equal (page 39)
- Move one duck from the bottom to the top.
- Move two ducks from the bottom to the top.
- ▲ Move two ducks from the third to the first.

From the Garden (page 41)
- 5 strawberries
- 4 tulips
- ▲ 8 tomatoes

Smiley Cupcakes (page 43)
- 8 cupcakes
- 12 cupcakes; 2 large boxes
- ▲ 1 large box and 2 medium boxes, or 2 large boxes and 1 small box

A Day at the Beach (page 45)
- 3, 2, 5 or 2, 3, 5
- 6, 4, 2, 1 or 6, 2, 4, 1
- ▲ 1, 3, 5, 10

Figure It (page 47)
- 5
- 8
- ▲ 3

At the Party Store (page 49)
(Note: students may write related equations and still be correct if it matches their thinking.)
- 2 balloons; $7 - 5 = 2$ or $5 + \square = 7$
- 7 candles; $13 - 6 = 7$
- ▲ 16 T-shirts; $9 + 7 = 16$ or $16 - 9 = 7$

Get a Prize (page 51)
- yo-yo and pencil
- yo-yo and toy car *or* two jump ropes
- ▲ yo-yo, toy car, and jump rope *or* 3 jump ropes

On the Line (page 53)
- 7
- 12
- ▲ 3 hops

Answer Key *(cont.)*

Which Numbers? (page 55)

- 6 + 3 or 3 + 6 = 9
- ■ 10 – 8, 12 – 10 = 2 (either equation may be first)
- ▲ 8 + 5 or 5 + 8 = 13; 12 – 8 = 4

Toss It (page 57)

Note: Both the addends and the possibilities may be written in any order.

- 2 and 4, 1 and 5
- ■ 1 and 8, 3 and 8, 5 and 8
- ▲ 2 and 8, 4 and 6, 4 and 8, 6 and 8

Where Did You Start? (page 59)

- 2
- ■ 6
- ▲ 10

Ask a Question (page 61)

Possible answers vary. One possibility is given for each number.

- 5: How many pencils do Ned and Sarah have together?

  1: How many more pencils does Ned have than Sarah?
- ■ 5: How many crayons and markers does Belle have?

  9: How many crayons and markers do Belle and Mark have together?

  1: How many more crayons does Mark have than Belle?

- ▲ 1: How many fewer erasers does Lexi have than Renaldo?

  5: How many erasers do Lexi and Renaldo have together?

  8: How many pencils do Lexi and Renaldo have together?

  0: How many more pencils does Renaldo have than Lexi?

How Many Animals? (page 63)

One, some, or all of the following ordered pairs may be listed.

- 1 and 7, 2 and 6, 3 and 5, 4 and 4, 5 and 3, 6 and 2, 7 and 1
- ■ 1 and 9, 2 and 8, 3 and 7, 4 and 6, 5 and 5, 6 and 4, 7 and 3, 8 and 2, 9 and 1
- ▲ 1 and 11, 2 and 10, 3 and 9, 4 and 8, 5 and 7, 6 and 6, 7 and 5, 8 and 4, 9 and 3, 10 and 2, 11 and 1

How Many Pennies? (page 65)

- 12 pennies
- ■ 8 pennies; 16 pennies
- ▲ 17 pennies

Hands, Toes, and Legs (page 67)

- 8 hands
- ■ Table: 20, 30, 40, 50; 50 toes
- ▲ Table: 4, 8, 12, 16, 20, 24; 24 legs

Show It (page 69)

- 11, 12, 21, 22
- ■ 16, 26, 36, 46, 56, 66
- ▲ 21, 31, 32, 41, 42, 43, 51, 52, 53

Answer Key *(cont.)*

Sticker Stories (page 71)

● Answers will vary but the two numbers must have a sum of 30.

■ Answers will vary but the second number must be 20 less than the first.

▲ Answers will vary but the sum of the first two numbers must be 40 more than the third number.

Tile Patterns (page 73)

● 47, 46, 45, 44, 43, 42 with 46, 44, and 42 shaded

■ 93, 92, 91, 89, 88, 87, 85, 84, 83, 82, 81, 80, 79 with 80 shaded

▲ 111, 109, 108, 107, 105, 104, 103, 102, 101, 100, 99, 97, 96, 95, 94 with 96 shaded

More or Less (page 75)

● Roberto; 42 > 36

■ Sophia; 60 < 62

▲ Carmen; 84 > 83; 83 < 84

Shrinking Machines (page 77)

● 30; subtract 10

■ 24; subtract 2

▲ 80; subtract 5

Number Stories (page 79)

● 6, 8, 93

■ 3, 2, 6, 8

▲ 7, 1, 29, 4, 26

T-Shirt Numbers (page 81)

● (from left to right) Mark, Jen, Loni

■ (from left to right) Manny, Sam, Ava

▲ (from left to right) Ann, Mini, Bailey, Joe

June Birthdays (page 83)

● June 29

■ June 16

▲ June 24

What Did You Buy? (page 85)

● 13 erasers

■ 1 box of Pirate Coins and 1 box of Pirate Treasures

▲ Note Cards and Birthday Cards; Thank-You Cards and Get Well Cards (*Note that either order of the two answers or the boxes within an answer is acceptable.*)

Ring Toss (page 87)

● 24; 34

■ 48; 68

▲ 4 rings (1 10-point and 3 1-point)

Favorite Numbers (page 89)

● 60

■ 58

▲ 52

What Is the Number? (page 91)

● 24

■ 14

▲ 36

Answer Key *(cont.)*

Number Groups (page 93)

● Possible answers include:

15: It is the only number with tens.

1: It is the only odd number with no tens.

■ Possible answers include:

61: It is the only number that does not end in 0 *or* it is the only odd number *or* it is the only number with an even digit in the tens place.

▲ Possible answers include:

2: It is the only number with no tens.

30: It is the only number you say when you count by tens.

17: It is the only odd number.

How Long? (page 95)

● blue; yellow

■ yellow; red; green

▲ yellow; red; blue; green

Find It (page 97)

● The second length should be circled.

■ The third length should be circled.

▲ The line drawn should be approximately 6 inches long.

Rod Lengths (page 99)

● Estimates will vary; 2

■ Estimates will vary; 4

▲ Estimates will vary; 5

What Time? (page 101)

● The first clock should be circled.

■ 6:30

▲ 4:30

What Happens? (page 103)

● home; dinner; bed

■ lunch; home; grandma's house

▲ game; gets up; breakfast

Finding Favorites (page 105)

● 6 children

■ 15 children

▲ 23 children

Make a Graph (page 107)

● apples

■ 9 toys

▲ 22 animals

Point Totals (page 109)

● 3 points

■ 13 points

▲ Tisa; 2 points

What Do We Know? (page 111)

Questions posed and answers given will vary, but should correspond.

First Names (page 113)

All answers may vary.

Answer Key *(cont.)*

What Shape Is Next? (page 115)
- ● ◯; circle
- ■ △; triangle
- ▲ ▢; square

What Shape Am I? (page 117)
- ● C
- ■ B
- ▲ D

Build a Design (page 119)
- ● 7 points
- ■ 8 points
- ▲ 11 points

Make It (page 121)
- ● ; 2; 2
- ■ ; 6; 2
- ▲ ; 5; 3

What Comes Next? (page 123)
- ● 4; 4
- ■ 10; 5
- ▲ 20

Shape Creatures (page 125)
- ● B
- ■ C
- ▲ A

Venn Diagram (page 127)
- ● 2
- ■ 3
- ▲ any figure with three or four sides with lengths that are not all the same

Tasty Treats (page 129)
- ● C
- ■ B
- ▲ A

References Cited

Bright, G. W., and J. M. Joyner. 2005. *Dynamic classroom assessment: Linking mathematical understanding to instruction.* Chicago, IL: ETA Cuisenaire.

Brown, S. I., and M. I. Walter. 2005. *The art of problem posing.* Mahwah, NJ: Lawrence Earlbaum.

Cai, J. 2010. Helping elementary students become successful mathematical problem solvers. In *Teaching and learning mathematics: Translating research for elementary school teachers,* ed. D. V. Lambdin and F. K. Lester, Jr., 9–13. Reston, VA: NCTM.

D'Ambrosio, B. 2003. Teaching mathematics through problem solving: A historical perspective. In *Teaching mathematics through problem solving: Prekindergarten–Grade 6,* ed. F. K. Lester, Jr. and R. I. Charles, 37–50. Reston, VA: NCTM.

Goldenberg, E. P., N. Shteingold, and N. Feurzeig. 2003. Mathematical habits of mind for young children. In *Teaching mathematics through problem solving: Prekindergarten–Grade 6,* ed. F. K. Lester, Jr. and R. I. Charles, 51–61. Reston, VA: NCTM.

Michaels, S., C. O'Connor, and L. B. Resnick. 2008. Deliberative discourse idealized and realized: Accountable talk in the classroom and in civil life. *Studies in philosophy and education* 27 (4): 283–297.

National Center for Educational Statistics. 2010. Highlights from PISA 2009: Performance of U.S. 15-year-old students in reading, mathematics, and science literacy in an international context. http://nces.ed.gov/pubsearch/pubsinfo.asp?pubid=2011004

National Governors Association Center for Best Practices and Council of Chief State School Officers. 2010. Common core state standards. http://www.corestandards.org/the-standards.

National Mathematics Advisory Panel. 2008. *Foundations for success: The final report of the National Mathematics Advisory Panel.* Washington, DC: U.S. Department of Education.

Polya, G. 1945. *How to solve it: A new aspect of mathematical method.* Princeton, NJ: Princeton University Press.

Sylwester, R. 2003. *A biological brain in a cultural classroom.* Thousand Oaks, CA: Corwin Press.

Tomlinson, C. A. 2003. *Fulfilling the promise of the differentiated classroom: Strategies and tools for responsive teaching.* Alexandria, VA: ASCD.

Vygotsky, L. 1986. *Thought and language.* Cambridge, MA: MIT Press.

Contents of the Teacher Resource CD

Teacher Resources

Page	Resource	Filename
27–29	Common Core State Standards Correlation	ccss.pdf
N/A	NCTM Standards Correlation	nctm.pdf
N/A	TESOL Standards Correlation	tesol.pdf
N/A	McREL Standards Correlation	mcrel.pdf
130	Student Response Form	studentresponse.pdf
131	Individual Observation Form	individualobs.pdf
132	Group Observation Form	groupobs.pdf
133	Record-Keeping Chart	recordkeeping.pdf
N/A	Exit Card Thumbs	exitcard.pdf

Lesson Resource Pages

Page	Lesson	Filename
31	At the Farm	atfarm.pdf
33	Stacks of Blocks	stacksblocks.pdf
35	Draw and Count	drawcount.pdf
37	Lots of Apples	lotsapples.pdf
39	Make It Equal	makeequal.pdf
41	From the Garden	fromgarden.pdf
43	Smiley Cupcakes	smileycupcakes.pdf
45	A Day at the Beach	daybeach.pdf
47	Figure It	figureit.pdf
49	At the Party Store	partystore.pdf
51	Get a Prize	getprize.pdf
53	On the Line	online.pdf
55	Which Numbers?	whichnumbers.pdf
57	Toss It	tossit.pdf
59	Where Did You Start?	wherestart.pdf
61	Ask a Question	askquestion.pdf
63	How Many Animals?	animals.pdf
65	How Many Pennies?	pennies.pdf
67	Hands, Toes, and Legs	handstoeslegs.pdf
69	Show It	showit.pdf
71	Sticker Stories	stickerstories.pdf
73	Tile Patterns	tilepatterns.pdf
75	More or Less	moreless.pdf

Contents of the Teacher Resource CD *(cont.)*

Lesson Resource Pages *(cont.)*

Page	Lesson	Filename
77	Shrinking Machines	shrinking.pdf
79	Number Stories	numberstories.pdf
81	T-Shirt Numbers	tshirt.pdf
83	June Birthdays	junebdays.pdf
85	What Did You Buy?	whatbuy.pdf
87	Ring Toss	ringtoss.pdf
89	Favorite Numbers	favoritenumbers.pdf
91	What Is the Number?	whatnumber.pdf
93	Number Groups	numbergroups.pdf
95	How Long?	howlong.pdf
97	Find It	findit.pdf
99	Rod Lengths	rodlengths.pdf
101	What Time?	whattime.pdf
103	What Happens?	whathappens.pdf
105	Finding Favorites	favorites.pdf
107	Make a Graph	makegraph.pdf
109	Point Totals	pointtotals.pdf
111	What Do We Know?	whatdoweknow.pdf
113	First Names	firstnames.pdf
115	What Shape Is Next?	whatshape.pdf
117	What Shape Am I?	shapeam.pdf
119	Build a Design	builddesign.pdf
121	Make It	makeit.pdf
123	What Comes Next?	whatnext.pdf
125	Shape Creatures	shapecreatures.pdf
127	Venn Diagram	venn.pdf
129	Tasty Treats	tastytreats.pdf

Contents of the Teacher Resource CD (cont.)

Additional Lesson Resources

Page	Resource	Filename
52	Number Line 0–20	numberline20.pdf
58	Number Board	numberboard.pdf
72	Number Line 0–120	numberline120.pdf
74	Place Value Mat	placevalue.pdf
86	Ring Toss Template	ringtosstemplate.pdf
106	Flower Picture and Graph	flowers.pdf

Notes

Notes